ESCAPE
INTO
COTTAGECORE

HarperCollins*Publishers*
1 London Bridge Street
London SE1 9GF

www.harpercollins.co.uk

HarperCollins*Publishers*
1st Floor, Watermarque Building,
Ringsend Road
Dublin 4, Ireland

First published by HarperCollins*Publishers* 2021

10 9 8 7 6 5 4 3 2 1

© HarperCollins*Publishers* 2021

Ramona Jones asserts the moral right
to be identified as the author of this work

A catalogue record of this book is
available from the British Library

ISBN 978-0-00845878-2

Printed and bound by PNB, Latvia

MIX
Paper from
responsible sources

FSC
www.fsc.org   **FSC™ C007454**

p.4, Author's own; p.9, Author's own; p.10 (right)
Rodolfo Marques on Unsplash, (left) Sarah Le on
Unsplash, (bottom) Alexandra Kikot on Unsplash;
p.19 Tomas Hudolin/Alamy Stock Photo; p.21,
Hamza Khan/Alamy Stock Photo; p.22 Tetra
Images, LLC/Alamy Stock Photo; p.26 (right)
Calatorescu/Alamy Stock Photo, (left) Eva-Katalin/
Getty Images, (bottom) Carolyn V on Unsplash;
p.29, V&A Images/Alamy Stock Photo; p.30 Rafael
Leao on Unsplash; p.33 Raychan on Unsplash;
p.37 Author's own; p.41 Annie Spratt on Unsplash;
p.45 (left) Evgeni Evgeniev on Unsplash, (bottom)
Gabriele Stravinskaite on Unsplash; p.49 Arthur
Edelman on Unsplash; p.50 Leora Dowling
on Unsplash; p.57, Author's own; p.60 (right)
Author's own; p.60 (left) Westend61/Getty Images;
p.78 DEEPOL by Plainpicture; p.81 Hamza Khan/
Alamy Stock Photo; p.83 (left) Plainpicture/
Juliette Chretien, (right) Betsie Van der Meer/
Getty Images, (bottom) Thomas Barwich/Getty
Images; p.84 Markus Spiske on Unsplash; p.85
Plainpicture/Elektrons 08; p.86 Mikroman6/Getty
Images; p.88 Plainpicture/Stephen Shepherd;
p.105 V&A Images/Alamy Stock Photo; p.106
Author's own; p.111 Plainpicture/Heidi Mayer;
p.125 NightandDayImages/Getty Images; p.128
(left) ClarkandCompany/Getty Images; p.133
Plainpicture/Caterina Rancho; p.135 DEEPOL
by Plainpicture/Anna Kern; p.139 Author's Own;
p.146 (right) Author's Own, (left) plainpicture/
Caitlin Strom; p.155 Annie Spratt on Unsplash;
p.166 Sanuar Aktar on Unsplash; p.173 Annie
Spratt on Unsplash; p.176 Tyler Nix on Unsplash;
p.183 Christin Hume on Unsplash; p.187 DEEPOL
by Plainpicture/Alberto Bogo; p.196 (left) Sophie
McAulay/Alamy Stock Photo, (bottom) DEEPOL
by Plainpicture/ Debby Lewis-Harrison, (right)
Plainpicture/Narratives/Emma Lee; p.203
DEEPOL by Plainpicture/Emil Fagander Pages 14,
42, 39, 45 (right), 60 (bottom), 64, 65, 67, 69,
73, 75, 76, 90, 93, 95, 101, 102, 108, 114, 115,
117, 119, 128 (right and bottom), 136, 143, 146
(bottom), 149, 153, 157, 161, 162, 165, 167, 178,
180, 189, 191, 193, 195 and all illustrations
© Shutterstock.com

ESCAPE
INTO
COTTAGECORE

*Embrace cosy
countryside comfort
in your every day*

RAMONA
JONES

HarperCollins*Publishers*

CONTENTS

INTRODUCTION

INTRODUCTION

I can thank my granddad for my love of nostalgia. Whenever
my mum needed a break from the combined demands of
childrearing and office life, she would drop my little sister
and me off at Granddad's gate, and we would stay at his place
for the weekend. Every creaking floorboard and dusty vintage
book there was a comfort, and I knew we'd be in for a few days
of magic and exploration. It wasn't uncommon for the other
grandchildren to end up there too. Together, the six of us would
rummage through the attic in search of antique treasure and
my grandma's old vintage dresses, sneak off to neighbouring
orchards and pinch apples, round up the geese and collect
their eggs for breakfast. And if it was raining, we would huddle
around the range cooker and exchange anecdotes and tales.

School was difficult for me. I struggled with sensory and
social issues and minimal support, and by the time I reached
secondary school, my mental health was at a crisis point.
All through this time, I knew I would be safe when I got to

Granddad's house. I could play in the garden on my own without judgement, or lose myself in a storybook while Granddad kept the fire stocked with logs. It was a haven from the rest of the world and the first place I felt truly able to be myself.

Granddad's place somehow managed to lag behind advances in technology. When mobile phones became the norm, they wouldn't work in his village. Broadband lines were installed for many of us, but not for him. My cosiest memory is of staying in an old pine bed in 'the Blue bedroom' as a teenager. I realised that due to the lack of signal, there was no possibility of returning my friends' text messages, and I settled instead on watching the raindrops as they made patterns on the window. The ambient buzz of the house, the warm flicker of light from the lamp on the nightstand and the occasional hoot of an owl took me away from my stress and lulled me into a gentle calm. Having no choice but to observe, I learned how restorative nature, solitude and quiet could be.

Although my memories of being dropped off at Granddad's house are a few decades old now, they still bring me the same sense of enchantment. I've woven as many strands of them into my adult life as I possibly can: I still replenish lost energy with walks in nature, I search flea markets for dresses reminiscent of my grandma and I decorate my home with old books and antiques that bring me a gentle reminder to live slowly and intentionally. With these actions, I restore a sense of safety that the world can otherwise deplete me of.

In today's fast-paced times, where productivity is valued over contentment, many of us are longing for old-fashioned comforts and a safe space to explore our identities. That's where Cottagecore comes in.

Cottagecore isn't about moving to a large estate in the country, nor is it a title that's earned from owning land. Cottagecore is an internet aesthetic, inspired by the nostalgia of rural life. It values traditions such as crafts, baking, preserving the natural world and caring for others. As Cottagecore was founded by the LGBQTIA+ community, it seeks to make a safe space where pastoral comforts can be enjoyed by all. Imagine a life where you avoid all of your stresses, relocate to a fairy-tale cabin in the woods and write your own narrative among nature. That escapism is the essence of Cottagecore – taking comforting aspects of the past and tying them in with a modern existence to create a sense of magic and escape.

Cottage life has had many different meanings throughout its history. The earliest cottages of medieval England were built on the grounds of manor houses as residences for workers, who would work full time to comply with orders from the lord of the manor. These early cottages were simple dwellings, built from local materials and designed to meet only the most basic of needs. There would have been a smallholding for the owner to raise animals or grow food and medicinal herbs, but there was no scope for the fanciful decorations and colourful cottage gardens that we know today. The goal of the cottage dweller at this point was survival, so there really weren't any frills attached to the lifestyle.

Life for the cottager had begun to look more promising by the sixteenth century, when Queen Elizabeth I set about improving the lives of the poor. Many comfortable timber-framed English cottages were built during her reign. It is these that come to mind when we think of idealised rural life – a modestly sized detached dwelling with exposed timber beams, tall chimney stacks extending from the hearth, charming timber-framed windows, a thatched roof and a garden full of trees, shrubs and herbs. The sort of cottage we might think of as belonging to a fairy tale or bedtime story. This provided the origins for the romanticised view of cottage life.

By the eighteenth century, cottages were built to house miners and weavers, designs were sophisticated, but functionality was still a priority. Cottages were often built to a 'two-up, two-down' plan, meaning two rooms upstairs and two rooms downstairs, and terraced building was common.

From the Victorian era, industrialisation and mass production freed cottage owners from the need to be self-sufficient. Many people abandoned their rural lives to work in the city. For those who remained, gardens became increasingly ornamental, and interiors more fashionable. Through this era, cottage life came to be associated with flowers, abundance and affluence.

The history of cottage life would previously have stopped here, but with the arrival of Cottagecore, we have been able to update things a bit. Cottage life is no longer reserved for those

who own a cottage. Instead, it is becoming a lifestyle or a hobby that can be enjoyed in both the city and the country. We are free to enjoy walks among trees, baking at home or listening to folk music. Cottagecore is about appreciating simple pleasures that bring us safety and joy.

By combining past and present, we can replace problematic and binary values, while maintaining an appreciation for the beautiful – whether that's a love of vintage fabric, growing herbs on a windowsill or simply finding the time to read a book in an outdoor space. Thankfully, we have also gained the ability to capture and share our love of the whimsical through cameras and social media, which has inspired many to add a little Cottagecore into their own experience.

This book isn't about uprooting your life in the city and settling off-grid in the middle of nowhere; nor is it about an unattainable or prescriptive lifestyle. It's not even about living in a cottage. It's an exploration of the different aspects of Cottagecore, including relaxation, home decorating, style, gardening, food, travel and community. It will help you to notice seasonal change and rekindle your love for nature. You are free to experiment with as many or as few ideas as you wish. But let them bring you a nostalgic sense of joy as you escape into the magic of Cottagecore.

MINDFULNESS

MINDFULNESS

Many of us dream of moving to the countryside and escaping the rat race of working life. We envision a slow lifestyle that's full of simple and rewarding tasks. Instead of our morning commute, we might stroll through a garden and collect eggs from a chicken coop. The day would be structured around walks in nature, and in the evening we might cosy up by the fireside. The aim being to escape stress and feel connected with nature and the present moment.

Cottagecore is about bringing this sense of peace and contentment into our everyday lives, wherever we find ourselves. Thankfully, there are plenty of ways we can connect with the present moment and feel more grounded.

Mindfulness is built upon teachings of the Eastern world and has roots in a number of religions. Many Western authorities in mindfulness learned from Buddhist teachers, and some therefore consider mindfulness to be a simplified representation of sati, the first step towards enlightenment in

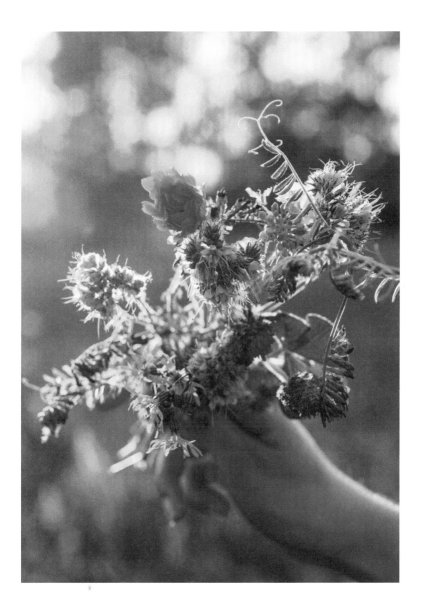

Buddhism. Sati has a broad meaning within Buddhism. It has been translated to encompass a number of elements, generally summarised as concentrated attention. Although in the West we often practise mindfulness as a discipline in its own right, it is important to remember that its origins lie within religion.

Mindfulness can be practised in a number of ways, from simple breathing exercises to guided forest bathing (the Japanese ritual of being calm and quiet among the trees, while breathing deeply – see p. 126). The overall goal is to bring your attention to the present moment without judgement, to let go of the past and to stop worrying about the future. Mindfulness is a practice of observation and acceptance. There are so many benefits associated with it. Studies have shown that it has the ability to reduce symptoms of stress, depression and anxiety. Just a short session can have long-lasting, positive effects on the way we experience the world.

Because we approach mindfulness without judgement, we should try not to get too hung up on the end result. Instead, we should allow ourselves to experience the process without focusing too much on our skill level.

'Do not dwell in the past, do not dream of the future, concentrate the mind on the present moment.'

– Buddha –

Breathing exercises

The most straightforward form of mindfulness requires nothing but your breath. Breathing exercises are useful tools for combatting stress and anxiety, and grounding yourself in the present moment. They provide a sense of connection between the mind and body that often gets lost among the chaos of modern life. Once you have tried these exercises a few times, you will always have them with you to use whenever you need a moment of calm and connection.

To ease yourself into breathing exercises, begin with a couple of minutes per day. You can increase this amount of time as you desire, and practise at multiple moments throughout the day, whenever you feel your body or mind needs it.

You can do these exercises either seated or lying down. If you are seated, place your feet flat on the floor and roughly hip-distance apart. With your palms facing upwards, rest one hand on top of the other in your lap. Imagine there is a string pulling you up from the crown of your head; this will help you to settle into a comfortable posture – you want to lengthen the spine and relax the shoulders.

If you're lying down, move your arms slightly away from your body and face your palms up. You can either lie with your legs straight or bend your knees so that your feet are flat on the floor. Avoid wearing tight clothes that might interfere with deep breathing.

Pursed lip breathing

This exercise enables you to easily take control of your breath. The deliberate control will allow you to slow your rate of breathing and feel more relaxed. It's a useful exercise for providing immediate relief when you are feeling stressed or overloaded.

1. Sit or lie down in a comfortable position (see p. 23). You may prefer to close your eyes.

2. Relax your head, neck and shoulders.

3. Close your mouth, and inhale through your nose for two counts.

4. Purse your lips as though you are about to whistle.

5. Exhale through your pursed lips for four counts.

6. Continue with this pattern for as long as you wish.

Belly breathing

This exercise helps to restore a connection with your body. It can allow you to feel more grounded in yourself and in the present moment, and it may also help to reduce the amount of effort required of your body while it breathes. It's a useful tool for times when your thoughts are running wild and you need to collect yourself.

1. Sit or lie down in a comfortable position (see p. 23). You may prefer to close your eyes.

2. Rest your left hand on your belly and your right hand on your heart.

3. Find a gentle breathing rhythm through either your nose or mouth.

4. Pay attention to the rise and fall of your chest as you breathe. You may notice more movement in your ribcage and less in your belly. Encourage your breath movements to fill your belly by moving the area as you breathe.

5. If you notice yourself getting distracted, gently return your attention to the rise and fall of your belly.

6. Continue with this pattern for as long as you wish.

Equal breathing

Equal breathing means inhaling and exhaling in equal measure, which helps you to relax and enhance your focus. Feel free to increase the breathing counts to achieve a deeper breath, provided your inhale is as long as your exhale.

1. Sit or lie down in a comfortable position (see p. 23). You may prefer to close your eyes.

2. Inhale slowly through your nose to the count of three.

3. When you are ready, exhale slowly through your nose to the count of three.

4. Continue with this pattern for as long as you wish.

A mindfulness
bath ritual

A long soak in a warm bath is a sure way to relieve stress and muscle tension and calm an overactive mind. There are a few little indulgences you can add to your bath to create a relaxing sensory haven.

Essential oils are a great-value way to personalise your bath ritual. These are highly concentrated, so you will need only a few drops and a small bottle will last for months. Each type of oil brings a different quality (see p. 28), so you can tailor your bath to your needs, whether you want to relax, invigorate yourself or simply enjoy a favorite scent.

Paying attention to the scent of your chosen essential oil is also a useful focal point for practising mindfulness. All you need to do is guide your attention towards the scent. If you notice your thoughts drifting to other things, gently bring your focus back towards the scent again.

Before using an essential oil in the bath, be sure to dilute it with a carrier oil. This will ensure that it doesn't cause irritation. Vegetable-based oils are great for this; you might want to try almond, grapeseed or olive oil. Mix one tablespoon of carrier oil with five to fifteen drops of your chosen essential oil. You can either add this mix to the bath just as you are about to get in or try massaging the oil mix on to your skin beforehand.

Essential oils for the bath

* **Lavender:** promotes relaxation and restfulness and is often used as a sleep aid. As such, it is a wonderful oil to use in an evening bath as you unwind and get ready for bed.

* **Lemon oil:** an invigorating scent that can be used to regain energy, boost mood and reduce stress. Lemon oil is also used to reduce pain. There is plenty of value in this powerful essential oil.

* **Chamomile:** can be used for relieving anxiety and promoting restfulness, which makes it another relaxing option to use in an evening bath ritual. Chamomile can also be used to settle nausea and ease irritation from skin conditions such as eczema.

* **Ylang ylang:** often used in perfumes or aromatherapy thanks to its beautiful fragrance, this oil has calming effects on mood and can assist in lowering both blood pressure and heart rate. A few drops of ylang ylang oil will transform your bath into a calming oasis.

To complete your bath ritual, adorn the room with candles to create a relaxing ambience. You can also add two handfuls of Epsom salt to the water, to help ease muscle pain and tension.

'Lord, make us
mindful of the little
things that grow and
blossom in these days
to make the world
beautiful for us.'

– William Edward Burghardt Du Bois –

Gratitude journaling

Taking a few moments to write down what you are grateful for is a really great way to appreciate life's simple joys. Keeping a regular gratitude journal is a wonderful mood booster and will help to protect your wellbeing during stressful times. If you build this practice into your routine, you will experience gratitude at the moment of writing, as well as gaining a prolonged sense of appreciation throughout the day, while your journal is held in the back of your mind.

Gratitude journaling tips

The act of writing something down brings enhanced focus and helps to create a lasting memory. It's a great idea to keep your journal in a physical notebook, rather than a phone or tablet, as this will deepen your experience.

Keeping a gratitude journal with a partner or family member is a fantastic way to appreciate things you may not have noticed before, or to recall positive experiences you'd forgotten about. If you both work through the same prompts (see p. 32) and then compare answers, you'll discover lots to be grateful for.

If you find yourself stuck for inspiration, remember the little moments: perhaps you spotted a sweet dog on your walk to work, or you noticed the colours of autumn emerging on the trees.

The easiest way to make a routine for your gratitude diary is to stick with a consistent structure and a regular writing time. For example, you might keep a notebook by your bedside and list 'five things you were grateful for today' right before you fall asleep. Simplicity and regularity are the tools that will really ingrain your new habit.

Our brains organise our memories during sleep, so writing this journal before bed is a sure way to develop a grateful way of thinking.

Here are twenty prompts to help you on your way with gratitude journaling:

1. What is something you enjoyed today?
2. What is something you are looking forward to?
3. What is your happiest memory?
4. Who are you grateful to have met in your life, and why?
5. Where is your favourite place?
6. Where do you feel safe?
7. What is your favourite season, and what do you like about it?
8. What personality traits are you glad you have?
9. Which of your recent social interactions are you grateful for?
10. Which friends do you most value?
11. Which musicians are you glad exist?
12. What are your favourite family memories?
13. What do you like about where you live?
14. What is your favourite sound?
15. What is your favourite taste?
16. Describe your favourite pet and what you liked about it.
17. When was the last time you laughed, and what made it happen?
18. Have you ever received a random act of kindness?
19. Have you ever provided a random act of kindness?
20. Describe a time when you felt truly at peace.

Once you've got the hang of these prompts, try thinking of some of your own. You'll realise there is so much to be grateful for.

These are just a few ways for you to welcome the practice of mindfulness into your life. The key is to find a routine that works for you. A little bit of daily practice will bring long-term relief and resilience to stress. Regular mindfulness allows you to see beauty in the simple things, providing you with a strong foundation to help you endure whatever life throws your way.

HOME

HOME

When we think of cottage interiors, we think of an eclectic mix of vintage and antique furniture, a happy clutter where every item has a story to tell. Building materials are often exposed – perhaps a wall of brickwork, a flagstone floor, a stone fire surround or timber beams running along the ceiling. Raw materials are cherished and celebrated, warps in wooden floorboards are welcome, for they allow us to imagine the pottering of feet across the years. Old buildings have stories to tell, and we want them to be told.

The aim of Cottagecore is to recreate the safe and cosy vibe of an old cottage in our homes, regardless of whether our space is old or new. It doesn't have to be a major renovation. A comfy armchair, a vintage floor lamp and a stack of old books will provide a welcoming reading nook in the corner of a room, and can make you feel like you're relaxing in a cabin that's nestled in the woods.

The phrase 'one man's trash is another man's treasure' certainly holds true here. For those who are choosing to

modernise their homes, their antique and vintage furniture becomes a hindrance in need of removal. With a quick search on Facebook Marketplace or eBay, you should be able to find some bargains nearby. Bulky items such as armchairs, sofas and tables can often be found at low prices, where folks are in a hurry to get rid of the old and bring in the new. Using search terms such as 'vintage', 'antique', 'shabby', 'Victorian' and 'farmhouse' should give you a good place to start when looking online. For the best deals, try second-hand shops, vintage fairs, flea markets and house-clearance businesses.

Beyond saving money, another great reason for buying second-hand is sustainability. When we buy something new, we exploit resources such as wood or cotton, oftentimes via unethical labour and habitat destruction. Creating and transporting new goods has a large carbon footprint, too, especially when we consider the short lifespan if an item is thrown away after a few years. By buying second-hand, we both avoid creating something new and prevent something old going to waste.

You'll also find that vintage items are built to last. These days, items are often designed to break or go out of fashion – this is known as planned obsolescence, and it ensures that we keep spending money. The older the item, the better chance it was created with craftsmanship and timeless design in mind; if it has lasted for the best part of a century so far, you'll likely have many more happy years with it. And if you needed any more reasons to shop second-hand, vintage shopping is way more exciting than buying new! Your items will likely be one of a kind and hard to mimic.

'Home is the
nicest word
there is.'

– Laura Ingalls Wilder –

Cottagecore
interior checklist

Here are some classic Cottagecore furnishings to look out for on your hunt for vintage treasure. Don't worry if you find objects that are a little worn – that only adds to their charm!

* Needlework cushion covers (and plenty of cushions)
* Pine dressers, sideboards, shelves and farmhouse tables
* Chintz curtains and fabrics
* Voile curtains
* Porcelain ornaments such as Staffordshire dogs
* Fairy lights
* Wooden or brass candlesticks
* Old oil paintings
* Baroque-style picture frames
* Vintage books
* Wicker baskets and trugs
* Striped or microprint wallpaper
* Matt, water-based wall paint
* White cotton tablecloths and doilies
* Vintage cutlery
* Mismatched ornaments and memorabilia
* Record players and vinyl
* Dried flowers

* Rocking chairs
* Chandeliers and lanterns
* Oriental rugs
* Vintage floor lamps
* Wool throws and blankets for chairs, sofas and beds
* Grandfather clocks
* Iron or French-style bedframes
* Antique sofas or chaises
* Armchairs and snugs
* Wreaths
* Vintage china such as Blue Willow or Asiatic Pheasant
* Linen or cotton bedspreads, eiderdowns, quilts, ruffled valances and voile or cotton bed canopies

Houseplants

A houseplant is an easy way to breathe a bit of Cottagecore
into your living space. Houseplants can improve mood and
reduce stress. There are plenty to choose from, and many are
low maintenance. In the cottage spirit of being both ornamental
and purposeful, some houseplants – such as mint or lavender –
are useful in the kitchen, too.

Boston fern

The Boston fern is a plant that was popularised by the
Victorians. It's fantastic for bringing some green into your
indoor space. This fern is suited to a room with less direct light.
As the Boston fern loves humidity, it is especially well suited to
a bathroom, but you can keep it happy in most rooms, as long as
you water it regularly and mist occasionally.

Pelargoniums

Pelargoniums, also known as indoor or scented geraniums, are a generously flowering houseplant. They are native to South Africa and became a popular feature of the European country home during the Victorian era. Pelargoniums are easy to look after; they are drought tolerant, so be sure not to overwater them. They love the sun and are not cold hardy. They will do best on a sunny windowsill.

Pelargonium flowers and leaves are edible and richly scented; they make great decorations for salads and cakes. The essential oils found in pelargoniums, which can be purchased, are also said to relieve anxiety and depression, as well as deterring insects such as mosquitoes and wasps.

One of the most appealing things about pelargoniums is the enormous range of colours and sizes available. Whether you love large plants and bright colours or dainty pastel flowers, you can be sure to find a variety to suit your indoor space.

Lemon tree

If you have the space and light available for a lemon tree, you'll benefit from both its beautiful, evergreen foliage and the occasional lemon harvest. The Meyer variety of lemon tree (roughly 3–4m tall, requiring a 3–4m space around it) is well suited to indoor growing. If you have a porch or conservatory, or if your place has large windows that get at least eight hours of direct sunlight per day, you can welcome a lemon tree or two into your home. They are a little more work than other houseplants, but you can't beat a lemon drizzle cake made with home-grown lemons!

Myrtle topiary

Myrtle topiaries are a fantastic way to add a bit of formality and class to your living space. A neatly clipped topiary evokes images of stately homes or the gardens of a French chateau. The scented leaves of myrtle can also be used in cooking, making it a multifunctional houseplant. Myrtle plants require full sun, so they are perfect for conservatories, porches and balconies. They also like cold conditions and would prefer a space away from central heating.

Herbs

An indoor herb garden brings the perfect mix of beauty
and functionality. Many herb varieties are rooted in cottage
history thanks to their medicinal properties and culinary uses.
Herb gardens can also be incredibly economical – you can grow
herbs in tin cans, as long as you've cut a small drainage hole at
the bottom. Many herbs – such as mint, rosemary and thyme
– will root from cuttings: after you've bought a packet of fresh
herbs from the supermarket, place three or four lengths of
about 10–15cm in a cup of water, ideally on an indirectly lit
windowsill. After a week or so, you should see tiny white roots
appearing from the submerged part of the plant. When you
notice your cutting has rooted, go ahead and plant it in a small
container or tin of potting compost, and soon enough you will
have a selection of free plants!

Perennial herbs such as mint, rosemary, thyme and oregano
don't need to be regrown every year, so they are particularly
great value and low maintenance. As long as you're not too
greedy with picking from them, they should grow happily
and through the long term. Herbs such as parsley, basil and
coriander have a shorter lifespan and will need to be replaced
after a few harvests, but they are easy to grow from seed.

Ivy

There's nothing like an ivy plant to evoke a fairy-tale image. Ivies are known as prolific growers in the garden, but by containing them in a pot, you'll have a rewarding houseplant that grows quickly without overtaking your space. Ivy plants need a decent amount of natural or artificial light – a windowsill with indirect sunlight is perfect. If you get a lot of light throughout your room, they look enchanting trailing across a bookshelf.

Cut flowers

Cut flowers are a cottage staple. Vintage milk jugs or stoneware pots make great vases. For smaller bunches, an old jam jar will do just fine. If you don't grow flowers at home, you may want to pick up a bunch from your nearest supermarket or greengrocer. Alternatively, you can look for foraged blooms, such as ox-eye daisies or cow parsley.

Photographing
interiors

Once you're satisfied that your interior has captured the
Cottagecore charm, it's time to share the magic on social media.
Whether you're using your smartphone or professional camera
gear for interior photography, there are a few things you can do
to really bring the space to life.

The first and most important rule is to pay attention to
the light in a room. Unless you are going for an evening glow,
natural and diffused daylight will do the best job at highlighting
your space, and you should try to keep artificial lights switched
off. Experiment with pulling back curtains or blinds to get as
much natural light into the space as possible. Adding mirrors
and reflective surfaces to dark corners will help to soften
shadows. If your room is in direct sunlight, you may struggle
at midday when the sun is at its highest point – shooting at this
time can result in strong shadows that make details hard to see.
Instead, try early in the morning, late afternoon or a cloudy day.
Because all rooms are different, it's important to pay attention to
light changes throughout the day to find the time that works best
for your space.

Before taking that photograph, it's worth tidying up a bit.
To complete the vintage feel, you may want to hide modern
appliances such as TVs or games consoles (unless there is a way
to seamlessly integrate them into your space). Tuck away exposed

wires and hide smaller bits of clutter, such as laptops and magazines. There is an acceptable amount of clutter within the Cottagecore vibe, though, so a simple tidy up should suffice.

Don't be afraid to play around with layout. In a living room, you might have sofas and chairs set up for optimal television watching, and that's fine, but it may not be optimal for photography. Take a few photos using the original layout, move things around a bit and then take another photo and compare. Keep playing around until you find an arrangement that photographs well.

From a technical perspective, bear in mind the following:

* **It is often best to shoot interiors dead on** – perhaps best popularised as the Wes Anderson angle. You want to stand directly opposite your subject and hold your camera at around chest height. Try to capture some symmetry, straight lines or balance within the frame, as this will appear pleasing to the eye.

* **If you find yourself in a smaller space, you can try using a wide-angle lens**, or wide setting on your phone, if that's an option. This will showcase as much of your space as possible. Failing that, don't be afraid of photographing details and close-ups.

* **Cottages are typically small, dark and pokey spaces – by nature, they are really difficult to photograph.** It can be very rewarding to spend some time styling a little, cosy scene – perhaps a cup of tea and an open book on the edge of an

armchair. You'll be surprised by how few details are needed to create a welcoming, rustic mood in a photo.

* **The easiest way to edit your photos is through apps.** The VSCO app provides a selection of filters based on analogue film. You can also use the grain, vignette and fade tools to emulate vintage photography. Another popular editing tool is Snapseed – best for editing specific parts of your photos; for example, you can use the brush tool to increase exposure in poorly lit areas.

Overall, when it comes to taking photos, every shot has value. If you shoot your space and it doesn't look right, it's a lesson learned. Spend some time experimenting until you find a way to capture that magical Cottagecore mood. Every great photographer started somewhere, so try to enjoy the journey!

Cottagecore interiors are playful, busy and happily cluttered. There is plenty of space to experiment and show off your personality. Before mass production, cottage dwellers would often stencil or hand-paint their walls, floors and shelves, and imperfections only added to the personality of the space. The more vintage items the better, though modern comforts are always a welcome addition. It's time to get thrifting, play around and, most importantly, have fun in the process.

FASHION

FASHION

Cottagecore fashion looks at the past through rose-tinted spectacles. Through linen pinafores, floral microprints and floaty dresses we might imagine ourselves as characters from *Pride and Prejudice* or *Wuthering Heights*. Dressing up with historical reference allows us to feel as though we are part of a classic novel, yet we write our own narrative and are not bound by former societal values.

There is a playfulness within Cottagecore fashion that allows you to truly express your identity. You can accessorise your Victorian-inspired frock with custom embroidery or embellishments – perhaps colour your hair brightly or adorn yourself with winged eyeliner and tattoos. Outfits that were traditionally assigned as either masculine or feminine can be combined or switched between. Cottagecore style can be an artform that showcases the spectrum of gender expression.

Just adding small elements of Cottagecore fashion can bring a comforting touch to your everyday outfit. A simple vintage accessory goes a long way.

Vintage outfit basics

There is loads of scope to experiment in Cottagecore fashion. Here are some styles to get you started.

Regency dress

If you've watched adaptations of *Pride and Prejudice*, then you will have seen a selection of Regency dresses, from the simple figure-highlighting day dress to the more extravagant ballroom affair. These dresses don't look out of place if you're visiting a stately home, formal garden or a nice hotel, and if you'd like to style some Cottagecore photos for your Instagram account, even better.

Features of Regency-style dresses include empire waistlines, a square or low neckline and small puffed sleeves. For formal use, these would have been 'dressed up' with a pair of silk gloves, pearl necklaces and waist ribbons. But without any of these accessories they are versatile dresses that could be worn in the day, particularly if they are neutral in colour and made of natural fabric. A Regency dress is the perfect way to add some Elizabeth-Bennet vibes to your wardrobe.

Prairie dress

The prairie dress is probably the style you'll see the most while browsing the Cottagecore hashtag on Instagram. If you've watched an adaptation of *Little Women*, you will recognise this style, characterised by high necklines, long sleeves and a full skirt, and often adorned with ruffles and frills. You can find prairie dresses made of light cotton for summer, or a heavier cord material, which is perfect for keeping warm in autumn, paired with tights and boots.

Smock

A smock is a relaxed-fit dress that tapers out from the neckline. There are plenty of modern smocks available, but occasionally you will find a vintage-style one that captures the Cottagecore aesthetic. Look for high or Peter-Pan collars, long or puffed sleeves, linen, light cotton or cord material and a floral, plain or microprint pattern. Pockets are always a bonus!

Pinafore and blouse

A pinafore is a full and sleeveless apron, often with buttons or a means of fastening at the back. It is a classic Cottagecore wardrobe staple. Paired with a linen or cotton ruffled blouse in a neutral colour, the pinafore is comfortable, practical and attractive. Look for linen or woollen pinafores, again in neutral colours, to create a historic cottager-style outfit, or cord/denim ones for a more modern adaptation.

Linens

Linen skirts, blouses and frocks are often available new. They are extremely comfortable and have great temperature regulation for hot summer days. Look for neutral colours and skirt designs with plenty of long, floaty fabric. Thanks to their light weight, linen dresses and skirts can be great for Cottagecore-styled Instagram shots: just give the skirt a swoosh and run slowly into the wilderness for perfect fairy-tale vibes every time.

Cloaks

Dressing to suit the Cottagecore style is much easier in warm temperatures, where just a long, cool dress will do. As the temperature drops and we need to wear more layers, it can be harder to recreate that fairy-tale mood. Cloaks are great for bridging this gap. A shorter cloak that's similar to a poncho is quite easy to style into a modern outfit. And a long cloak with a large hood works fabulously if you're going all out with the fantasy image.

Dungarees

A good pair of dungarees will see you through the practical side of a Cottagecore life, particularly if you're interested in outdoor activities. Dungarees can be accessorised with long, lace-up boots, a frilly blouse and a vintage locket to bring in a touch of historic influence without going full-blown cottager. In colder weather, pair your dungarees with a heavy wool pullover for the ultimate in cosy comfort.

Cords and tweed

A few cord or tweed items in your wardrobe is another way to get through the colder months without compromising on your country-inspired look. A pair of high-waisted cord trousers teamed with a shirt and waistcoat makes for a winter outfit that's perfect for walking or gardening.

Blouse and jeans

A good, ruffled blouse can be teamed with jeans or shorts for a modern Cottagecore twist. If you're out in public and you don't want to commit to a full Victorian smock, a vintage Edwardian-style blouse should do the trick.

Cottagecore accessory box

Accumulating a few of the following items allows you to either add a subtle hint of vintage to an everyday outfit or to complete a full prairie-inspired costume.

* Straw hat
* Silk handkerchief
* Vintage watch or pocket watch
* Vintage leather belt and gloves
* Tweed hat
* High lace-up boots
* Frilled socks
* Tartan or ribbed socks
* Vintage locket
* Vintage brooch

* Vintage glasses
* Tweed or tartan tie/bowtie
* Woven straw handbag or basket
* Floral choker necklace
* Floral earrings
* Pearl necklace or headband
* Flower crown
* Hair ribbons
* Embroidered clothing

'Simplicity is
the ultimate
sophistication.'

– Leonardo da Vinci –

Sourcing your Cottagecore look

Thanks to the Victoriana revival of the 1960s–70s, historically inspired clothing isn't too difficult to source second-hand. Many vintage Victorian or Regency-style dresses are actually less than sixty years old, so they are still in quite good condition compared to their antique and original counterparts. Particularly in the 1960s, these country-inspired dresses, skirts and blouses were extremely well made, crafted from heavy cotton, linen or other natural fibres. Laura Ashley, a pioneer of the Victorian fashion revival, took print inspiration from wallpapers in the National Trust archives and other historic collections. She developed a romantic style of dress that was a breath of fresh air among modern styles.

Sourcing vintage clothes online

Online, you can source vintage outfits through eBay, Depop, Facebook Marketplace and occasionally Instagram if you follow vintage sellers. If you are buying from a vintage shop that has a curated style, you can expect a higher price tag. If you know what to look for on eBay or Facebook Marketplace, you'll have a better chance of finding a bargain from someone who is clearing out an old wardrobe.

As the Cottagecore movement has gained popularity, modern designers and small businesses have started making country-style dresses and linens too. For authentic styles, look for small businesses on Etsy that specialise in clothing for re-enactments. A search for 'custom prairie dress' should return some small designers. Buying dresses this way gives you control over sizes, cuts, collars, sleeve style and fabric choice, so you can choose dresses that are unique to you. It's also surprisingly inexpensive when compared to some of the designer Cottagecore styles.

Use the following search terms to track down vintage treasures online:

* Vintage
* Retro
* Prairie dress
* Linen
* Cotton
* Cottagecore
* 60s

* 70s
* 80s
* Regency
* Victorian
* Edwardian
* Gunne Sax
* Laura Ashley

Vintage shopping offline

Offline, you can source vintage outfits through second-hand or thrift shops, flea markets, vintage fairs, vintage shops and jumble sales. This method takes a bit more labour, but you are more likely to find a bargain, particularly if you are thrifting.

Cottagecore has started to find its way into fast fashion, though these designs are often poorly and unethically made, not created to last and have prints that are not quite as charming. If the option of buying second-hand or vintage is available to you, it's the most rewarding and sustainable route.

Photographing
Cottagecore fashion

* **As with many areas of photography, natural light is your best friend.** Try early-morning mist or golden hour for an extra layer of atmosphere.

* **If you don't have someone to help shoot your outfit for you, you can use a tripod and the timer setting on your phone or camera to set up your own shots.** It takes a little bit of practice to master posing and composition, but it is well worth the effort.

* **The key to photographing Cottagecore fashion is styling.** The easiest and most effective hack is to wear a skirt or dress that has plenty of fabric, and that flows well when 'swooshed'.

* **Pick a setting that complements the country outfit** – say, under a tree, in a field or sat at a vintage table.

* **Style your scene further with props**, such as a picnic blanket, vintage book or parasol.

* **Poses that don't connect directly with the camera can help to create a photo that's reminiscent of a vintage painting.** Try walking away from the camera, looking at something in the distance or engaging with a pet or a prop.

* **Edit your photos with a vintage-film-inspired filter**; the VSCO app is perfect for this (see p. 53)

Cottagecore fashion can be as minimal or as eccentric as you wish. It's a means of self-expression – by playing with your image you can play with your story, or simply add a little touch of nostalgia. If you have the option, searching vintage and second-hand shops for treasure can be incredibly fulfilling and your outfits will be one of a kind.

GARDENING

GARDENING

When you fall in love with gardening, you will always have something to look forward to on the horizon. Even in the depths of winter, you can plant a pot of tulip bulbs and watch every day as they build momentum towards their spring display. Gardening inspires connection among people and protection of the natural world: communities can come together to develop an allotment site or maintain or protect an undeveloped patch of land; you may exchange seeds or cut flowers with your next-door neighbour; or perhaps write to your local council and point out a green belt that could benefit from some trees or wildflower seeds.

Land ownership is not a prerequisite to feeling the joys of a garden. Plenty of plants and vegetables can be grown in pots on patios, balconies and windowsills – even on your dining-room table. Thankfully, many private gardens are open to visitors and can be found online. So if you don't take part in the gardening process yourself, you can still enjoy observing seasonal change in your spare time.

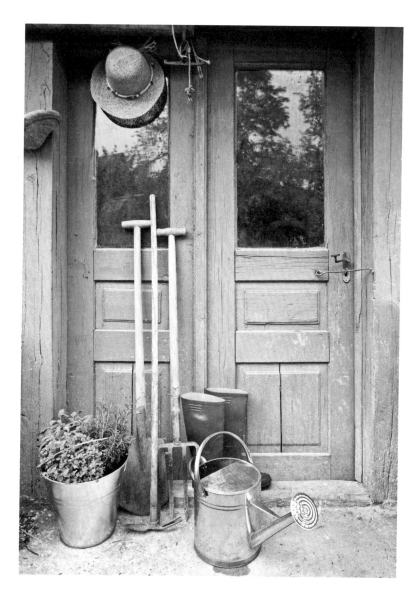

There are a number of reasons why you might want to garden. The health benefits are extremely well documented. From physical exercise and exposure to vitamin D to the release of mood-boosting endorphins, it's hard to find a reason why not to give it a go. If you are growing your own herbs or vegetables, these can make for nutrient-rich seasonal meals. They taste great, they're highly nutritional and don't rack up air miles in the way that imported produce does.

You might also want to garden for nature. As our insect population continues to decline, it becomes increasingly vital for us to plant habitats and food sources to offer them some protection. By welcoming in smaller creatures, we also welcome in biodiversity through the rest of the food chain. If we let snails into the garden, frogs might be partial to snacking on them. The frogs will attract birds, and the birds, in turn, attract foxes. As if by magic, there is a restored ecosystem at play, stemming from just a few plants. Finally, there is the soil. Our soil is the foundation of plant, animal and human health, and it is vital we take care of it. As plants decompose, they transfer carbon from the atmosphere into the soil, creating a 'carbon sink', whereby this carbon acts as food for the soil's ecosystems. With the right methods, we can use soil health to capture carbon and help us fight climate change.

'That is one good
thing about this
world . . . there are
always sure to be
more springs.'

– L. M. Montgomery –

Growing cottage flowers

When designing a cottage garden, window box or arrangement of pots, the key is to have something flowering in every season. This means there will always be a focal point, and your space will never look bare. The most challenging times are autumn and winter, when many trees and hedges shed their leaves, and few plants are in flower. There is still, however, a surprisingly large selection that blooms through this period to carry your display through. In bigger spaces, you can also use evergreen hedges, such as box and yew, to provide a backdrop through winter.

There are a few basics to get familiar with before we get started, but don't worry too much about learning all of the technicalities now. The easiest way to learn is by giving it a try.

Your flower display can be built from perennials, biennials, annuals and bulbs. If you are working in a patio or a garden, you may also want to add shrubs, hedges and trees to create structure.

Flower meanings

We might be familiar with sending red roses on Valentine's Day as a gesture of love, but these are not the only flowers with a deeper meaning. There are flowers to symbolise anything from love and passion to ambition and happiness – in fact, there is an entire language of flowers, known as floriography, and it is as rich as the human experience itself. Here are the meanings associated with some cottage favourites that you might like to add to your garden:

Calla lily (white) – purity and innocence

Daffodil (just one) – rebirth and new beginnings

Daffodils (a bunch) – joy and happiness

Gladiolus – remembrance

Hollyhock – ambition

Iris (purple) – compliments and wisdom

Iris (yellow) – passion

Iris (white) – purity

Lilac – youthful innocence

Mint – virtue

Rose (red) – love

Salvia (red) – forever mine

Snapdragon – deception

Tulip (red) – passion

Perennials

These are plants that flower every year, and as such, they can be a reliable confidence boost if you are new to gardening. Often, they will get bigger over time, and after a few years of growing perennials, you may be able to divide the plants, so you gain more for free. Perennials are usually herbaceous, which means the stems die back in the winter, but the roots will remain underground ready for the next growing season. Popular cottage perennials include delphiniums, peonies and catmint.

Biennials

Biennials are plants with a two-year lifecycle. In their first year, they will establish a basic structure of roots, stems and leaves. Then, they will flower in their second year, after which they will drop seeds. To maintain a yearly display of flowering biennials, you will need to add plants every year in preparation for flowering in the year to come. Popular cottage-garden biennials include foxgloves and hollyhocks.

Annuals

Annuals will flower and set seed within one year. Though the original plant won't return the following year, it will likely drop plenty of seeds that will give you new plants. You can use annuals to fill in the gaps in your display, or you could create a cut-flower area from them. Well-known cottage garden annuals include cosmos, poppies and cornflowers – all of which make great cut-flower displays to bring into your home.

Bulbs

A bulb is a plant that stores its life cycle in an underground, layered structure. Bulbs are usually perennial plants (they flower every year in the right conditions) that are either spring- or summer–autumn-flowering. Common cottage-garden bulbs include tulips and daffodils (spring-flowering) and gladioli and oriental lilies (autumn-flowering).

Shrubs

A shrub is a long-lasting plant with woody stems. Some shrubs are evergreen, while others lose their leaves over winter. Because of their rigid shape, shrubs are a good way to lend structure to your garden, and many flower generously too. Cottage favourites include buddleia, lilac and roses.

'To plant a
garden is to
believe in
tomorrow.'

– Audrey Hepburn –

Growing vegetables

Cottage gardens are typically a mix of productive and ornamental plants. Not only does this look beautiful, it also encourages biodiversity within your growing space, as flowers will bring pollinators into your space, and these, in turn, will pollinate your produce. Everybody wins!

Many vegetables are grown as annuals, so they produce food within the year they are planted and are then cleared away and composted. There are also perennial plants that give us a harvest every year, making them low maintenance and high reward. It's worth introducing a few of these into your space, so you will always have something to harvest.

Perennial crops for a low-maintenance vegetable garden

* Rhubarb
* Asparagus
* Jerusalem artichokes
* Globe artichokes
* Perpetual spinach
* Strawberries
* Summer and autumn raspberries
* Blueberries

Cottage-garden calendar

The following cottage-garden calendar will help guide you through the year. Of course, different locations have differing climates, so if you have mild winters in your area, for example, you may not need to lift tender plants in the autumn. It's worth looking into your garden 'zone' and its climate, as this will help you in making specific growing choices.

Spring

Spring is a generous and exciting season in the garden as life begins to emerge after a winter of rest. Your space may be blessed with blossoming fruit trees, tulips and daffodils will be in flower and it's the time to sow seeds for annual flowers and vegetables. It's the season of planning your garden year and getting into action.

Jobs for spring

* **Sow hardy annuals** (to flower this year) including baby's breath, sunflowers, sweet peas, cornflowers, poppies and night stocks. Hardy annuals can be sown directly into their flowering position in pots or beds, or they can be started in seed trays and transplanted as young plants.

* **Sow half-hardy annuals** (to flower this year) in a greenhouse or on a windowsill, including cosmos, zinnias, marigolds, nasturtiums and morning glory. These can be planted out after the last frost.

* **Harvest remaining crops** that were grown over winter, such as parsnips, sprouts and spring cabbage.

* **Sow tender vegetable seeds** in seed trays, including chilli, courgette, squash, pumpkin, tomato, leek and aubergine. These will need to be kept in a greenhouse or on a windowsill until the frost risk has passed.

* **Sow hardy vegetable seeds** directly into beds or containers, including beetroot, carrot, pea, radish, spinach, chard and turnip.

* **Plant out potatoes, onion sets** (immature bulbs – easier to grow from than seeds), shallots and garlic.

* **Plant out your tender** and half-hardy sowings in late spring.

What's in flower now?

Blossom * camellia * daffodils * tulips * bluebells * primroses * laburnum * irises * lilac * peonies * wisteria

Summer

Summer is when cottage-garden displays are usually at their peak. Blooms are abundant, pollinators are well fed and vases around the house are overflowing with cut flowers. Growth in the garden is at its fastest in summer, and many fruits and vegetables are ready to harvest. Be sure to take the time to admire your growing space while it is at its best.

Jobs for summer

* **Plant dahlia tubers** and autumn-flowering bulbs outdoors, in pots or beds where they are intended to grow.

* **Keep on top of weeding and watering.**

* **Deadhead spent blooms** or cut flowers for vases indoors; this will allow your plants to flower again (deadheading methods vary according to plant type, so it's best to check first how to do this).

* **Support large plants** that are at risk of falling over with wire frames or bamboo canes.

* **Sow perennial seeds**, including aquilegia, delphinium and lupin.

* **Sow vegetable seeds** directly into their growing location, including carrot, cauliflower, broccoli, spinach and radish.

* **Harvest fruits**, including early apples, berries, plums, figs and peaches.

* **Harvest vegetables**, including aubergines, tomatoes, beetroots, beans, courgettes and many more.

What's in flower now?

Delphiniums * peonies * foxgloves * azaleas * freesias * wildflowers * lavender * poppies * roses * sunflowers * dahlias * cosmos * catmint

Autumn

By autumn, the pace of growth in the garden has slowed down. Many trees are taken over with warm colours before they drop their leaves, and you can harvest hearty vegetables such as squash and pumpkin. While you are putting parts of your growing space to bed, you can begin to plan your spring bulb collections, planting daffodils and tulips to give yourself something to look forward to next year.

Jobs for autumn

* **Plant winter/spring bulbs**, such as daffodils, tulips, crocuses and snowdrops.

* **Protect tender plants** from frost by bringing them inside, mulching or storing in a greenhouse.

* **After the first frost, cut away the foliage from dahlia plants**. Lift and rinse the tubers, and then leave them to dry for a few days. Once the tubers are dry, overwinter them in a cardboard box of sawdust or compost, in an unheated space such as a shed or garage.

* **Lift gladiolus bulbs with a trowel**. Be careful to leave the foliage attached as this will feed the bulb. Wipe away any soil, then leave the bulbs to dry for a few days, before storing them in an empty cardboard box over winter.

* **Collect and compost fallen leaves**.

* **Harvest autumn produce**, including squash, pumpkin, carrots and autumn raspberries.

* **Sow seeds for cropping next spring**, including sweet pea, spring cabbage, onion and garlic. Note that some varieties will need protection from frost.

What's in flower now?

Dahlias * sunflowers * Japanese anemones * cosmos * marigolds * autumn ox-eye daisies

Winter

Winter is a time of rest for many plants. Contrary to what you may believe, though, there are still jobs to be getting on with in a winter growing space. While lots of plants are dormant, spaces are more accessible, making winter the perfect time to work on construction jobs, such as fixing your shed, building new raised beds or arranging a new collection of pots. There is also an assortment of winter vegetables to harvest. If you're lucky, you might have a home-grown Christmas dinner.

Jobs for winter

* If you missed out in autumn, **you can still plant your tulip bulbs** at the start of winter.
* **Work on construction jobs** and keep the garden tidy.
* **Harvest winter produce** such as chard, kale, cabbage, broccoli and Brussels sprouts.
* **There are still a few seeds you may wish to sow**, including winter salads, dill, parsley and broad beans.

What's in flower now?

Winter clematis * winter jasmine * cyclamen * snowdrops * hellebores * crocuses * camellia * hyacinths

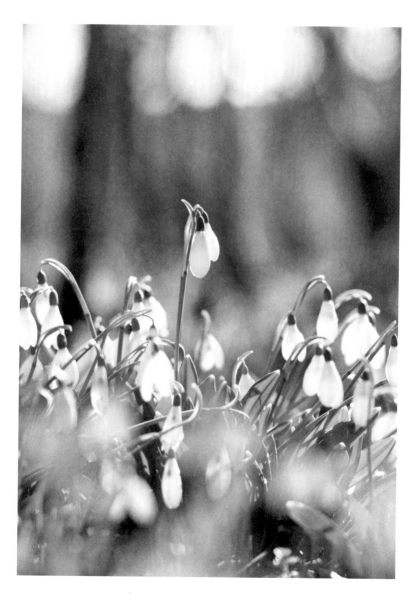

Upcycling in the garden

Accessorising your garden doesn't have to be expensive as there are plenty of quirky ways to upcycle things that would otherwise go to waste. This is eco-friendly and means your growing space will be original and unique.

Upcycled mini pond

You don't need a lot of space to create a pond for frogs or newts. If you can get your hands on a second-hand Belfast sink, half whiskey barrel or a small galvanised trough, it should do the trick. Make sure to plug any holes and then leave your pond out to collect rainwater (which is more wildlife-friendly than tap water). Oxygenating plants, such as hornwart and curled pondweed, will help to keep the water clear and algae-free, while aquatic flowers, such as water lilies and irises, can make your pond more ornamental. If you have a small pond, aim to place it in the shade, so the water doesn't evaporate in hot weather.

Bug hotel

You'll often see bug hotels (habitats for insects, particularly during hibernation) for sale in shops and garden centres, and they can be quite expensive. But most of what our insects need for a healthy hibernation exists in our gardens already. If you have some old pallets, it's even easier: stack a few of these on top of one another, or secure four pieces of wood together to create a thick frame. Then fill the gaps with dead wood, twigs, dry leaves, dry sticks and corrugated cardboard and place your 'hotel' somewhere it can sit undisturbed. The more bug hotels you have in your garden, the more you are doing to help protect valuable insect populations.

Pallet frame for climbers

If you want to grow climbing crops, such as pumpkin and squash, the best way to save space is by growing them vertically. Simply balance two pallets in an inverted V shape, secure them together with string or wire and your climbing plants will have a frame to grow on.

Beginners' gardening tips

* **Start with a couple of plants or vegetables that you absolutely love** – this will keep you motivated. Supplement these with a few plants that are easy to grow and highly rewarding, such as roses or radishes. They will give you a feeling of success.

* **Don't be afraid of failure**; some things will go wrong, but that's how we learn! There is still value in a lesson learned.

* **Similarly, nature has its own plan** – we can't always control it, but that can be a blessing. You may have some cottage-garden favourites that self-seed freely all over the garden.

* **Even the most proficient of gardeners still feel they have more to learn**, so try not to get too wrapped up in the big picture. There is an immense amount of joy in the smallest of flowers – try to focus on these details if things feel too much.

* **If you are growing crops, try to avoid growing the same plant in the same container two seasons in a row.** Crop rotation helps to prevent the soil from becoming depleted of specific nutrients or riddled with disease.

* **Avoid pesticides**, as they are harmful to natural and human health. Instead, aim to nurture a natural predatory cycle in the garden or growing space. If you discover aphids on your plants, don't spray them with pesticide. Leave them be, and

eventually, ladybirds will be attracted to the plant and will happily snack on the aphids. You could also plant a decoy plant, such as nasturtium or marigold. These are loved by aphids and will encourage predatory ladybirds to control the aphid population.

* **Neem oil** is another useful, natural pest deterrent to look into.

* **Frogs and newts are a great slug control.** Try introducing a pond or a small container of water to encourage frogs and newts into the space (see p. 94).

* **Look into companion planting** as another natural pest deterrent. For example, basil is a successful whitefly deterrent, and is often planted near tomatoes to prevent infestation.

* **Many plants will grow happily in pots.** Be sure to keep them watered in hot weather and use a good-quality, peat-free compost to give them nutrients.

It might seem there is a lot to learn in the garden, but the hardest part really is getting started. Once you get going and feel your hands in the soil, relaxation and enjoyment will take over, and you'll soon think there's nothing to worry about. There is as much joy in the process as there is in the end result (maybe even more). However big or small your growing project, let it bring you plenty of contentment.

FOOD

FOOD:
EATING AND COOKING
WITH THE SEASONS

Historically, cottagers would have eaten seasonally as part of their way of life. Produce would have been grown in a nearby plot, harvested fresh and then prepared over the fireplace. Though we might not have the means to be self-sufficient today, we know there are plenty of reasons to eat seasonal, local produce: you may want to take better care of your health, reduce food waste or adopt a more climate- and environmentally friendly diet. Or maybe you simply want to enjoy the taste of fresh ingredients.

How to shop seasonally

Many of us are interested in adopting more of a seasonal eating pattern but don't have the means to grow our own food, or at least not in a large enough quantity to be self-sufficient. Thankfully, there are a few things we can try to make the most of our local food supply.

To start, it helps to learn a little bit about what produce is in season throughout the year. This will give you an awareness of what to look for while you are shopping. If you want to make sure you're supporting local producers in particular, it's worth looking into the foods grown in your specific climate, month by month, as seasonal produce can vary significantly around the world. Here is a quick guide based on temperate growing conditions.

Spring

Asparagus * Beetroot * Broad beans * Cabbage *
Elderflower * Leeks * New potatoes * Peas * Purple sprouting
broccoli * Radishes * Rhubarb * Rocket * Spring greens
* Spring onions * Watercress

Summer

Apples * Asparagus * Aubergines * Beetroot * Blackcurrants
* Blueberries * Broad beans * Broccoli * Carrots * Cherries *
Courgettes * Cucumbers * Elderflower * Fennel * French beans *
Globe artichokes * Gooseberries * Loganberries * Mushrooms *
Pears * Peas * Plums * Radishes * Redcurrants * Rhubarb *
Runner beans * Shallots * Strawberries * Sweetcorn *
Tomatoes * Turnips

Autumn

Apples * Broccoli * Brussels sprouts * Cauliflower * Celeriac *
Chicory * Crab apples * Damsons * Jerusalem artichokes * Kale *
Parsnips * Pears * Pumpkin * Quinces * Sloes * Squash * Swedes *
Turnips * Wild mushrooms

Winter

Apples * Cabbage * Carrots * Celeriac * Celery * Forced rhubarb *
Jerusalem artichokes * Kale * Leeks * Parsnips * Pears * Pumpkin *
Purple sprouting broccoli * Swedes * Turnips

If you live in a city or only have a supermarket nearby, be sure to check the growing location on your produce. If this matches the country you live in, you'll know the produce is currently in season. It might take a little bit of time to get the hang of this, but you'll soon develop a habit, based on a rough idea of what to shop for during each season.

In the city, you may also have access to zero-waste shops for grains, flours, pulses and more. Many of these items store well, so buying them in a particular season isn't necessarily important. However, zero-waste shops will often source their products from ethical suppliers around the world and ensure their growers are paid fairly. There is plenty of value in that if you have the means to support your nearest zero-waste shop.

If you live in a more rural setting, look for nearby farm shops and markets, where you should be able to source local and seasonal produce. You may also have a greengrocer nearby. It's worth having a look around to assess the options. Note that you may still need to pay attention to the growing location of your produce, as some farm shops and greengrocers will import out-of-season items.

'One cannot think well, love well, sleep well, if one has not dined well.'

– Virginia Woolf –

Seasonal recipe ideas

Each season presents us with ingredients we can really celebrate. Whether it's a light rhubarb crumble in the spring or a hearty vegetable soup in the winter, there's something incredibly comforting about a meal made of fresh and local produce.

Spring
Rhubarb Peanut Crumble

Spring is rhubarb season, and what better way to celebrate
than with a classic rhubarb crumble with a peanut twist?
It's sweet and tangy, with a creamy and crunchy topping.

Serves 4 • Prep 15 minutes • Cooking time 20—25 minutes

Butter, for greasing

1kg (2lb 4oz/8¼ cups) rhubarb,
sliced

50g (2oz/¼ cup) caster
(superfine) sugar

2 tbsp cold water

1 tsp ground cinnamon

Cream, crème fraîche, ice cream
or custard, to serve

For the peanut-butter crumble:

100g (3½oz/1 cup) plain (all-
purpose) flour

50g (2oz/½ cup) rolled porridge
oats

50g (2oz/¼ cup) demerara
sugar

75g (3oz/generous ¼ cup)
crunchy peanut butter

50g (2oz/¼ cup) butter, diced

1. Preheat the oven to 190°C (170°C fan)/375°F/gas 5. Lightly butter
a shallow ovenproof baking dish.

2. Make the peanut-butter crumble: mix the flour, oats and sugar
together in a large mixing bowl. Break the peanut butter into
lumps and add to the bowl with the diced butter. Using your
fingertips, rub in the two butters until the mixture resembles
fine breadcrumbs.

. . . recipe continued overleaf

3. Mix the rhubarb, sugar and water in a bowl. Sprinkle with the cinnamon, and then tip the mixture into the buttered baking dish.

4. Sprinkle the crumble mixture evenly over the rhubarb, levelling the top, so the fruit is completely covered. Bake in the preheated oven for 20–25 minutes until the topping is crisp and golden brown and the filling is cooked and tender.

5. Serve warm with cream, crème fraîche, ice cream or custard. This also tastes good eaten cold the following day.

Variations

* *Make at other times of the year, using whatever fruit is in season — pears, apples, cherries, blackberries, plums, greengages, apricots or even strawberries.*

Summer
Basil Pesto

Basil plants will be thriving in the summer, and this pesto recipe is a quick and easy way to make the most of your harvest. Serve with pasta for a simple, seasonal lunch.

Serves 4 · Prep 5 minutes

50g pine nuts (2oz/⅓ cup), toasted
½ garlic clove
15g fresh basil (½oz/¾ cup), leaves picked
100ml (4fl oz/just under ½ cup) olive oil
Sea salt flakes
Freshly ground black pepper

1. Using a pestle and mortar, lightly crush the pine nuts until they begin to break down. Add the garlic to the mortar and crush again. Next, add the basil and half the olive oil, and continue to crush until the basil softens. You are looking for the leaves to break down and release their natural oils, but not quite so much that they begin to turn brown.

2. Transfer the contents of the mortar to a bowl and whisk in the rest of the oil, along with a generous pinch of salt and black pepper. Taste, and adjust the seasoning if needed.

Autumn

Roasted Beetroot

An autumn harvest isn't complete without a good stock of
beetroot. Here is a simple roasting method that can be
served as a light lunch or a side dish.

Serves 4 · Prep 5 minutes · Cooking time 30–40 minutes

450g (1lb/3⅓ cups) raw beetroot (beets),
peeled and cut into wedges
2 tbsp olive oil
1 tsp black mustard seeds
Balsamic vinegar, for drizzling (optional)
Sea salt

1. Preheat the oven to 220°C (200°C fan)/425°F/gas 7.

2. Toss the beetroot wedges with the oil and mustard seeds in a large
bowl. Place them in a roasting pan and sprinkle with a pinch of
sea salt. Cook in the preheated oven for 30–40 minutes, until
tender. Drizzle with balsamic vinegar (if using) before serving.

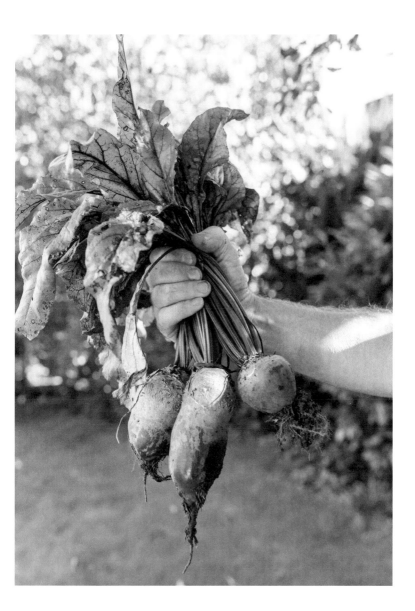

Winter

Creamy Brussels Sprouts Soup With Cheesy Croûtes

Brussels sprouts are often divisive – they seem to be a love/hate thing for many people. However, if you source fresh, in-season sprouts, you'll find it hard not to enjoy the flavour. Here is a comforting soup recipe to make the most of your harvest.

Serves 4 · Prep 15 minutes · Cooking time 35–40 minutes

2 tbsp olive oil

1 large onion, chopped

2 garlic cloves, crushed

300g (10½oz/2 cups) celeriac, peeled and diced

400g (14oz/3½ cups) Brussels sprouts, trimmed and halved

1 litre (1¾ pints/4 cups) vegetable stock

4 sprigs of thyme, leaves stripped

120ml (4fl oz/½ cup) crème fraîche

Sea salt and freshly ground black pepper

For the cheesy croûtes:

1 baguette, cut diagonally into 4 slices

2 tsp Dijon mustard

100g (3½oz/1 cup) grated Cheddar cheese

1. Heat the olive oil in a large saucepan over a low heat and cook the onion and garlic, stirring occasionally, for 8–10 minutes until softened but not coloured. Add the celeriac and cook gently for 2 minutes.

2. Stir in the sprouts and cook for 5 minutes. Add the stock and thyme leaves and bring to the boil. Reduce the heat to a gentle simmer and cook for 15–20 minutes, or until the vegetables are really tender.

3. Blitz the soup in a blender until smooth – you can do this in batches. Return to the pan and season to taste with salt and pepper. Stir in the crème fraîche and reheat gently.

4. Meanwhile, make the cheesy croûtes: lightly toast the baguette slices under a hot grill (broiler). Thinly spread each slice with mustard.

5. Pour the soup into 4 heatproof bowls and float the baguette slices, mustard-side up, on top. Sprinkle with the grated cheese and pop under the hot grill for just long enough to melt the cheese. Serve immediately.

Variations

* *Top with crumbled crispy bacon or pancetta for a non-vegetarian version.*
* *Use a large potato and 2 celery sticks instead of the celeriac.*

'Good food is the
foundation of
genuine happiness.'

– Auguste Escoffier –

Baking

Herby Halloumi Scones

The humble scone is a cottage classic. This savoury recipe uses herbs and halloumi for a perfect lunchtime treat.

Makes 6 scones • Prep 15 minutes • Cooking time 10—15 minutes

225g (8oz/2¼ cups) self-raising flour, plus extra for dusting

1½ tsp baking powder

½ tsp salt

½ tsp English mustard powder

50g (2oz/¼ cup) butter, diced, plus extra for greasing

1 tbsp black mustard seeds

A few sprigs of mint, finely chopped

125g (4½oz/1 cup) grated halloumi, plus extra for sprinkling

1 medium free-range egg, beaten

90–100ml (3–4fl oz/⅓ cup) milk, plus extra for brushing

2 tbsp sesame seeds

Cayenne pepper, for dusting

1. Preheat the oven to 220°C (200°C fan)/425°F/gas 7. Lightly butter a baking tray (cookie sheet).

2. Sift the flour and baking powder into a large mixing bowl. Mix in the salt and mustard powder, then rub in the butter with your fingertips until the mixture resembles fine breadcrumbs. Stir in the mustard seeds, mint and halloumi.

3. Using a spatula, gently stir the beaten egg into the flour and cheese mixture, together with enough milk to form a soft dough. Add more flour or milk, if necessary, to make it stick together without being too dry or too wet.

4. Dust a clean surface with flour and gently roll out the dough about 2cm (¾in) thick. Use a 6cm (2½in) fluted cutter to cut out rounds. Roll out the leftover dough and cut out some more rounds, so you have approximately six scones.

5. Place the scones on the prepared baking tray and brush them with milk. Sprinkle with sesame seeds and a little grated halloumi. Bake in the oven for 10–15 minutes until risen and golden brown.

6. Dust with cayenne and leave to cool slightly before serving warm. You can split and butter them, if wished.

Make your own jam

Jam is a great way to prolong your summer berry harvest, whether you grow raspberries yourself or pick up a few punnets from your local farm shop. If jam is canned correctly, it can store safely for months.

Homemade Raspberry Jam

Raspberry jam is the perfect sweet pick-me-up for those cold winter mornings, making a great Christmas gift for your friends and family too.

Makes 1 large jar or 2 smaller jars · Prep overnight · Cooking time 35 minutes

450g (1lb/4 cups) raspberries
450g (1lb/2¼ cups) white jam sugar
Zest and juice of 1 lemon

1. The night before you make the jam, combine the raspberries and sugar in a large bowl, cover and set aside.

2. When you are ready to make the jam, put a plate in the freezer. Pour the macerated fruit into a large saucepan, making sure to scrape all the sugar and juices from the bowl. Add the lemon zest and juice and place the pan over a low heat and cook until all the sugar has dissolved. Turn the heat up to high and simmer for 5–10 minutes until the jam is thick, stirring occasionally to prevent it from sticking.

3. To test if the jam is ready, remove the plate from the freezer and drop a teaspoon of jam onto it. Once it is cool, press it with your finger – it should wrinkle. If it is too runny, return to the heat for a few minutes until you reach the wrinkle stage.

4. Remove the pan from the heat and scrape off any scum from the top. Leave to cool slightly for 20 minutes, then ladle the jam into one large or two smaller sterilised jars. Seal immediately and allow to cool completely. Store in a cool, dark place. Once open, keep in the fridge.

How to photograph your food

Once you've prepared your food, it's time to share it with the world on social media! Firstly, you need to make sure you are making the most of natural light. You'll want to set up a food photography area next to a window, where the natural light is soft. You may find the light is too harsh at midday, in which case you should experiment with shooting in the morning or late afternoon. If the light is too strong, there will be very dark shadows and very bright highlights in your image, and it might be difficult to make out the details. Diffused natural light will evenly expose your subject with a gentle glow.

One of the most exciting parts of food photography is styling. With good styling, the camera is almost an afterthought – you can create stunning visuals with your phone camera alone if you get the set-up right. Think about your backdrops. Try to use a surface that isn't too reflective. Old scaffolding planks, reclaimed wood, tabletops and even specialist food photography backdrops will help to set the mood of a rustic farmhouse kitchen. If you don't have much space for reclaimed wood, you can purchase vinyl food-photography backdrops that roll up into a cardboard tube.

It's always worth keeping an eye out for vintage props while you're in second-hand shops or visiting car boot sales;

they really do add magic to your photographs. Decorate your scene with props such as china saucers, cake stands, interesting glasses, linen napkins and vintage cutlery. These will help to recreate a rustic setting.

Two of the most popular angles for food photography are top-down (also known as the flatlay) and dead-on (directly facing the subject). You will notice that some foods will be much easier to shoot from a particular angle. Cake, for example, is often easiest to shoot dead-on because of its height. In contrast, a bowl of porridge and berries is often easier shot as a flatlay, as this will show details of the food and scene more clearly. Play around with both angles and see which works better for your subject.

Whether you are growing your own produce, stocking up at the local farmers' market or checking the supermarket shelves to see what is in season, there is always a way to make the most of your local food supply. Nothing is better in taste or more gratifying to cook with than freshly picked fruit and vegetables.

OUTDOOR
LIFE

OUTDOOR LIFE

Beyond life at home, there are plenty of other ways we can bring a little bit of Cottagecore into our experience through the great outdoors. You may be interested in hiking and outdoor sports. Perhaps you enjoy walking your dogs through woodlands and meadows. Or maybe you simply enjoy the peaceful feeling of noticing the fresh air on your skin.

Green spaces allow us to get back in touch with the simple things and connect with nature. Research has shown that the presence of green spaces in urban settings reduces stress and anxiety and prolongs life expectancy via increased physical activity and improved mental health. It's no wonder there is a rising use of ecotherapy to tackle the stress of modern life. There have even been studies on green micro-breaks, showcasing the incredible healing power of a technology-free short break in the forest.

Forest bathing

Forest bathing is a Japanese relaxation technique, known in Japan as *shinrin yoku*. It is an act of mindfulness. Through the simple act of observing nature under a canopy of trees, there are a number of positive effects on the body, including reduced stress, lowered blood pressure and increased immune function. The positive effects of forest bathing are so well documented that a number of GPs have started recommending the practice as a means of boosting patients' wellbeing.

If you enjoy woodland trails, or perhaps you walk a dog regularly, you may wonder whether you have unintentionally enjoyed the act of forest bathing before. However, one key feature is intentionality – to go to the forest or green space with relaxation in mind. This means a distraction-free visit. No dogs, no phones and no rush.

Once you have rid yourself of possible distractions, you can be guided entirely by your senses. Pay attention to what you see, hear and smell. Instead of following a map, follow your senses with curiosity, and take everything in. Beyond relaxation, there is no agenda.

Beginners may find a guided forest-bathing session helpful. When you first pay attention to your sensory experience, distraction is inevitable, but a guide will help you return your attention to your senses. They may slow your walking speed down or direct you to a particular pattern or texture.

Here are some tips for self-guided forest bathing:

1. Choose a quiet woodland location, outside of peak visiting times if possible.

2. Allocate two to three hours so that you don't feel rushed (though note that a few minutes of practice is still beneficial if you are pushed for time).

3. Turn off your phone and put it out of immediate reach in a pocket or bag.

4. Slow down your walking speed – and remember, this is an act of observation rather than exploration.

5. If you find a comfortable place to sit, take a seat. Being still may encourage birds and other observable wildlife into the area.

6. Work through your senses one by one. What can you hear? Are there any textures you want to touch? What do they feel like? Can you feel warmth or fresh air on your skin?

7. Check in with your breathing. If it's fast, try taking a few deep breaths to slow down the rhythm. This will help you feel more relaxed.

Foraging

A popular theme within the Cottagecore aesthetic is collecting food from the wild landscape, better known as foraging. Heading into the wilderness with a small woven basket is reminiscent of a fairy tale and has become a popular part of the escapism that Cottagecore has to offer.

There are plenty of foods we can collect from the wild, as long as we are responsible with how we treat nature through the process. It's also important to pick the correct plant to ensure it is safe and edible. Some wild foods, such as mushrooms, can be poisonous and hard to identify, and so should be left to the experts. Make sure you take photographs and descriptions with you, and if you are in doubt about something, don't pick it.

The most obvious value of foraging is the result – free food – although there is also immense benefit in the process of exploring nature, paying attention to detail and seasonal change and enjoying our own presence in the outdoors. Foraging allows us to think about where our foods come from and how they may sit within an existing ecosystem. If you enjoy foraging, you may also wish to support a charity that protects native woodlands and hedgerows, in order to give something back to nature.

The following is a basic guide; it's worth looking into foraging in your local area, too, as different regions will have differing landscapes. Again, remember to take a guide or image references with you to ensure you are picking the correct foods, respect the guidelines of landowners and be sure if you are picking weeds that they haven't been sprayed with chemicals beforehand.

Spring foraging

As nature reawakens from her winter rest, there are lots of wild foods to be found in spring.

Dandelions

Dandelions are easy to identify and are widespread in meadows and gardens. Look for the bright yellow rosette of petals. All parts of the dandelion are edible and can be used either raw or cooked as part of a recipe. Try making dandelion honey or dandelion tea with the yellow flowers, or a salad with the young leaves.

Nettles

Nettles are another common plant in gardens and meadows. Though they are sometimes considered a weed, they are in fact a superfood. Nettles are rich in iron and vitamins A and D. Pick with gloves to avoid stinging. You could try nettle tea, soup or even sautéed nettles as a side dish.

Wild garlic

Wild garlic can be found in damp and shady woodlands and hedgerows. You'll know when you've found it thanks to its strong aroma. Both the leaves and flowers of wild garlic are edible, but you'll find the most efficient method is to collect as many leaves as possible. Wild garlic is a versatile ingredient. You may want to try making wild garlic pesto, butter or bread.

Summer foraging

Many plants are at their best in summer. Hedgerows are lined with blackberries, and edible flowers are blooming with abundance. There is a bountiful harvest for those who venture into nature with a basket.

Elder
When using elder, you want to be sure you are only using the flowers and berries (the rest of the tree is toxic). Elderflowers have a beautiful, fresh flavour and scent and are great in teas, syrups and liqueurs.

Wild strawberries
If you're not able to grow your own strawberries, fear not! You may find wild ones – also known as alpine strawberries – growing among woodlands and hedgerows. It's unlikely you

will get a large harvest, so enjoy your freshly picked strawberries straight from the plant.

Blackberries

Blackberry picking is one of the most popular foraging methods of the present day, and for good reason. There are plenty of these delicious berries to be found in hedgerows, so you should be able to fill a basket with ease. Blackberries are rich in vitamin C and are a great ingredient in juices, crumbles and pies.

Autumn foraging

As flowering comes to an end and trees shed their leaves, many plants are left bearing edible fruits that are a treat to forage.

Sloes

If you are out on an autumn walk, you may come across blackthorn bushes covered in thorns and bright blue sloes. These sloes can be used to make wine and gin, or jam and jelly. You can also use the leaves of the blackthorn bush to make tea.

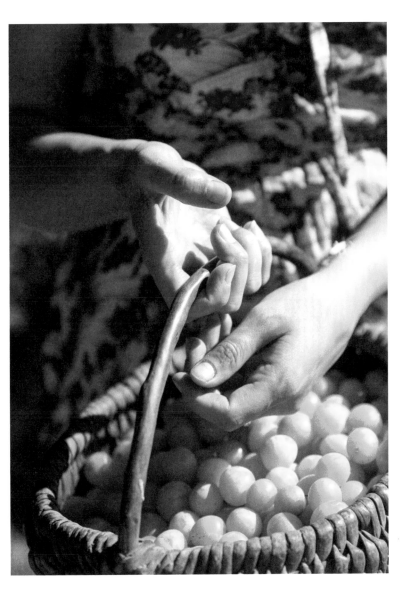

Wild raspberries

You may come across wild raspberries in woodlands and hedgerows in early autumn. If you are lucky enough to find a large crop, you can use them as you would store-bought. If the crop is small, enjoy them straight from the plant as a fresh and tasty snack.

Winter foraging

Though winter is the most difficult season for foraging, there are still wild foods to collect. If you know what to look for, you can find a rewarding harvest.

Sweet chestnut

Chestnuts are a festive favourite, and a large tree should give you a plentiful crop. Try roasting chestnuts on an open fire for a tasty Christmas tradition. Alternatively, you may want to try adding them to salads or stuffing.

Hairy bittercress

Though typically considered a weed, hairy bittercress is a peppery herb that makes a fantastic addition to salads and sandwiches. You could also use it to add flavour to pesto or soup.

Pick your own

If foraging isn't an option, you may be able to find a local farm with a 'pick-your-own' facility. Often these are aimed towards young children, but they are becoming increasingly popular with teens and adults too, as more of us are developing an interest in rural pleasures. From spring, you may find tulip-picking events, in summer, look for strawberry and apple picking and in autumn, you'll be sure to find a pumpkin patch that's open for picking.

Travel guide

Spending more time outdoors allows you to really value the beauty in seasonal change. You can revisit the same spot throughout the year, and each time find a new detail to appreciate. Alternatively, you could curate a travel bucket list based on seasonal details. Here are a few suggestions to get you started.

Spring

Bluebells in the woodlands of **Europe**
Cherry-blossom festivals throughout **Japan**
Tulip fields in the **Netherlands**

Summer

Lavender fields in the **South of France**
English country gardens in the **Cotswolds, England**
Fairy-tale castles in the **Scottish Highlands**

Autumn

Glorious autumn colour in **New England, USA**
Gothic fairy-tale castles in **Rhine, Germany**
Idyllic autumn scenes in **Snowdonia, Wales** (don't miss
Tu Hwnt Ir Bont)

Winter

Snow-covered mountains in **Hallstatt, Austria**
Winter activities in **Banff National Park, Canada**
Christmas celebrations in **Rochefort-en-Terre, France**

Photography tips for the great outdoors

Inspired by historic country living, classic novels and paintings from a bygone era, outdoor spaces are a fundamental part of Cottagecore imagery. Using the timeless backdrop of nature is perfect for staging a cottage-inspired photoshoot.

The most important point here is to look for locations. Meadows make for a simple but effective scene. Better still, you could seek permission to use a field of wheat or lavender (lavender farms often allow members of the public to explore within certain hours). You can also look for unspoiled historic towns or villages and let the fabric of the old buildings set the scene for you.

Try to avoid hints of modern life, whether parked cars, crowds of visitors, telephone lines or modern architecture. If you choose a green space in a city, you might want to look for individual details within it, rather than using the area as a whole – for example, framing your shoot around an ancient tree or a flowering shrub.

As always, light is key. If you want to create a moody feel, take your pictures in the rain or on a grey or overcast day. The most romantic of shoots will be in the golden hour after a glorious day of sunshine, or try morning mist for a sense of enchantment. As a general rule, sunshine from lunchtime into early afternoon is the most difficult light to work with. If you find yourself shooting in the middle of a sunny day, it might help to work in dappled light, under a tree perhaps.

Props will help you to add the finishing touches. If you are creating a travel-themed shoot, you could try using vintage luggage. If you are out foraging, take a woven basket with you and fill it to the brim with wild foods and flowers.

Connecting with nature is at the heart of Cottagecore. Thankfully, there are a number of ways to appreciate the great outdoors. If you are pushed for time or unable to travel, you can still find plenty of joy in observing a green space on your way to work, or paying attention to the gardens, trees and window displays in your neighbourhood. Even just a little bit of nature will do your mind a lot of good.

HERBOLOGY

HERBOLOGY

Herbs have a longstanding history in cottage life. The earliest of cottages would have had some sort of herb garden for entirely practical purposes, and many medicinal uses are still relevant today. A number of these have now been proven by science, while others remain trusty old wives' tales. There are many simple ways to welcome herbal remedies into your routine – herbal teas, for example, are plentiful in supermarkets and easy to use, or you can buy essential oils for use in massage, to drop into your bath or a diffuser. So if you find a herbal remedy that improves your experience, it is worth making the most of it. You can grow herbs and medicinal plants in a garden or on a windowsill, or you can buy prepared herbal products in various forms at your local health store.

A basic guide to herbology

Here is an overview of popular herbal remedies and medicinal plants.

Remember to consult a health professional if you wish to use herbal medicine. Herbal remedies can have side effects and/or interact with over-the-counter and prescription medicines. So always speak with your doctor first.

Aloe vera

Aloe vera gel has natural cooling and soothing abilities that make it especially useful for treating itching and swelling. As such, it is often used to treat sunburn, insect bites and eczema. Aloe vera gel can also be used as a natural moisturiser, as it is rich in vitamins C, E and beta carotene, which are associated with anti-ageing.

How to use: harvest aloe vera gel from mature plants that are a few years old. Use a clean, sharp pair of scissors or a knife to remove two to three large leaves from the outside of the plant;

cut at the base of the stem and ensure the leaves are free of mould. Hold each leaf with the cut end downwards and allow any yellow liquid to drain out. Discard the liquid. Wash the leaves and trim off any spikes. Lay the leaves flat and fillet off the skin to expose the gel layer. Remove all skin and yellow gel, until you are left with clear gel only. This can be applied directly on to the skin as a topical moisturiser or treatment. If you want a smooth application, you can blend the aloe vera gel, and then strain through a layer of muslin. Apply the liquid directly to the skin and discard the pulp from inside the muslin. Alternatively, aloe vera products can be purchased from health and beauty stores.

Chamomile

Chamomile is best known for its calming and anti-anxiety properties, though it boasts many other uses, including use as an anti-inflammatory, for pain relief and for swelling reduction. As a plant, chamomile is a cottage-garden favourite, and you can grow your own with ease for plentiful summer harvests. Preserve your chamomile flowers by hanging them indoors, upside down to dry – this will provide you with a year-round supply.

How to use: infuse fresh or dried chamomile flowers in hot water for tea; or for direct healing to swelling, place a handful of chamomile flowers in the centre of a piece of fabric, pull the corners together and secure with an elastic band, then dip in water and place against the skin as a compress. Chamomile can also be purchased as an essential oil. After diluting with a neutral carrier oil (see p. 27), you can massage the oil into your skin or add a few drops to your bath.

Echinacea

Echinacea is a cottage-garden favourite for its long-lasting and colourful cone-shaped flowers. Native Americans have used echinacea for centuries to treat a number of ailments. Today it is known for its ability to stimulate the immune system and it is used to relieve symptoms of colds and flu, and to soothe minor cuts and grazes.

How to use: echinacea is available to purchase from health stores in tea, tablet, liquid or ointment form. As various parts of the plant can be harvested, the potency of each product is different and dosage will vary across individual supplements.

Feverfew

Feverfew was awarded its name thanks to its early use in treating fevers. Today, it is used in the form of tea or supplements to prevent migraines and arthritic pain. It can also be used as an insect repellent. Feverfew may interact with other medications, so you should consult a health professional before using it medicinally. With its dense, daisy-like blooms, feverfew is another cottage-garden favourite. You can easily grow your own and then dry to preserve.

How to use: if you don't grow your own, feverfew is available in a supplement form from health food shops. Alternatively, you can infuse 1–2 teaspoons of fresh or dried feverfew leaves in a cup of boiling water to brew tea.

Garlic

Garlic has a number of uses: it improves cholesterol levels, which may help to lower the risk of heart disease; it is used to fight off the common cold, thanks to its dense nutritional value; and it

'If country life is healthful to the body, it is no less so to the mind.'

– Giovanni Ruffini –

has also been shown to reduce oxidative stress, which may lower the risk of brain diseases, including dementia. Thankfully, garlic is widely used in the kitchen, so it is quite easy to include in your routine.

How to use: garlic can be bought as a supplement from health food stores, though the benefits of these are contested. Research suggests that garlic cloves are best used fresh, after being cut or crushed. If you can incorporate 5–12 cloves into your daily meals, you will be making the most of it. Garlic is easiest to digest when roasted whole. Roasted garlic has a more subtle and caramelised flavour, so you may find it more tasty too: leave the skin on your garlic bulb, slice and discard the top quarter of an inch or so, then place the bulb on a sheet of foil, drizzle with olive oil, wrap in the foil and roast in the oven at 200°C (180°C fan)/400°F/gas 6 for 30 minutes.

Ginger

Ginger is famous for its anti-sickness and anti-inflammatory qualities and its ability to soothe the digestive system. It is often used as a remedy for morning sickness in pregnancy, or for alleviating period pain within the first few days of menstruation. Ginger can also have positive effects on circulation, as well as encouraging perspiration during colds and flu. Ginger roots and powdered ginger are readily available in supermarkets and greengrocers. If you save a section of the root, you can plant it in a pot of compost and grow ginger as a houseplant. Once your plant is established, you can harvest more of the roots for consumption.

How to use: there are various ways to include ginger in your diet. You can use freshly grated roots in meals, such as curries and stir-fries, or infuse thin slices in boiling water to brew tea. You may find it easier to use in cooking in powdered or pickled form.

Lavender

Lavender can be used to reduce stress and anxiety, and to encourage sleep. Lavender plants can be grown in a garden or on a windowsill, and then hung upside down to dry. Lavender is also a useful pest deterrent – putting a few sprigs in the pockets of your clothes can help to discourage pesky clothes moths, while rubbing diluted lavender oil onto your skin may keep mosquitoes and other biting insects away.

How to use: you can use 1–2 teaspoons of fresh or dried lavender flowers in a cup of boiling water to brew a calming tea.

Alternatively, you can store dried lavender flowers in a small cotton bag under your pillow to provide a soothing scent at bedtime. You can infuse a jar of neutral oil such as almond or argan oil with lavender flowers for at least a week, following which the oil will become beautifully scented and can be used as a homemade alternative to lavender essential oil. Otherwise, you can buy the essential oil from a lavender farm or health store. This will need diluting with a carrier oil before use, as it is very potent.

St John's wort

St John's wort is a wild plant with a long history of being used as a natural antidepressant. It is also sometimes used as a treatment for mild anxiety, seasonal affective disorder and sleep disturbances.

Note: St John's wort interacts with many medicines, including other forms of antidepressants and birth-control pills, so it should only be taken in conjunction with guidance from a health professional.

How to use: St John's wort is available as an over-the-counter supplement in many health stores.

Tea tree

The tea tree is native to Australia. Its oil can be used as a cleanser and sanitiser, as it kills a number of common bacteria, viruses and fungi. Tea tree oil is often used as a treatment for mild acne and skin conditions or to cleanse small wounds or insect bites.

How to use: tea tree oil can be purchased as an essential oil. As this is highly potent, you should dilute it with a neutral carrier oil before use, particularly if you have sensitive skin. You can also add a few drops of diluted tea tree oil to your bath. Do not consume, and avoid contact with eyes and ears.

Valerian

Valerian is a wild plant that grows among grasslands. The root is dried and used as a sleep aid and a relaxant; it was used historically in ancient Greece and Rome to treat headaches and trembling.

How to use: the easiest way to use valerian root is to purchase a tea blend with valerian as an ingredient. If you look for night-time teas in health food stores you are likely to find one. Alternatively, you can purchase dried valerian root, and infuse 1–2 teaspoons in a mug of boiling water to make your own tea. Consume this about an hour before sleeping.

Easy herbs to grow for tea

There are plenty of easy-to-grow herbs that can be used to make a cup of tea. To preserve your harvest, hang a bunch of your home-grown herbs upside down from the ceiling to dry out. This will supply you with herbal teas until the next harvest season.

Your tea can be made with either fresh or dried herbs. To make it, simply infuse 1–2 teaspoons of one of the following in a mug of boiling water and consume when it reaches a comfortable temperature (the part of the plant most commonly used in herbal remedies is mentioned in brackets):

* **Chamomile (flowers)**
* **Fennel (seeds)**
* **Feverfew (leaves)**
* **Lavender (flowers)**
* **Lemon balm (leaves)**
* **Peppermint (leaves)**
* **Rosemary (leaves)**

All of the above can be grown in pots and will reflower year on year.

Hopefully, you have found a herbal tea or remedy to grow or enjoy. Herbs and plants hold incredible properties – from early cottage gardens to modern medical usage, it's no wonder they have such a longstanding medicinal history.

MAGICK AND
ENCHANTMENT

MAGICK AND ENCHANTMENT

There is an air of enchantment within Cottagecore. For some, this means a journey into the world of magick and witchcraft. For others, it means taking inspiration from fairy tales and fantasy in the way they view the world.

The realms of magick and witchcraft are rich and wonderful to explore. You might try your hand at tarot reading or crafting spells, or perhaps pay attention to the cycles of the sun and the moon, and the way these affect nature around you, or your mind and body.

You might wish to follow a more general path towards enchantment; through noticing details in nature, finding simple pleasures and nourishing your inner child.

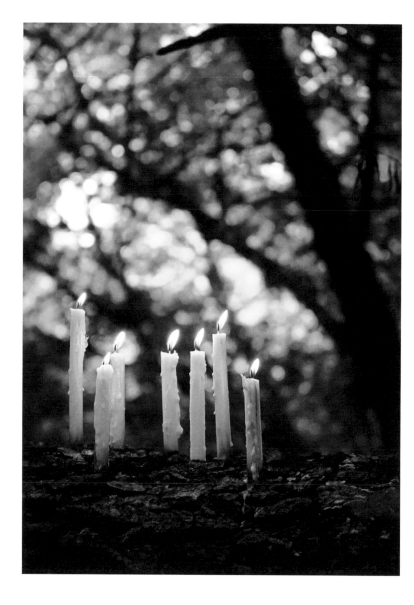

Magick

The term magick, with a 'k', is widely used to differentiate the practice of spiritual magick from the card tricks and staged illusions that we have grown to associate with the term 'magic'. Many of those who practise magick believe in karma – the notion that 'you get what you give'. In this case, spells are not used to cause harm, as an individual can bring harm upon themselves through their own maladaptive choices. Magick is a neutral term – in itself, it is neither good nor bad – the intention being determined by those who practise it.

Magick practised outside of Wicca is tailored to the individual. There are no firm rules on how it is used, and many practitioners will also abide by another religion. For many young people who have been raised into an inflexible societal structure, magick provides a sense of freedom, expression and escape from rigidity.

The beauty of this approach is that you are free to explore as many or as few approaches as you'd like. Here are a few ideas to introduce you to magick.

Dream journal

As soon as you wake up, if you remember your dream, write it in a journal. This helps you to tap into your subconscious thoughts. You will be able to understand your deepest desires, hopes, fears and insecurities. The more you do this, the more likely you will be to remember your dreams in future.

Equinox and solstice

Equinox and solstice are astronomical occurrences that determine seasonal transition. During equinox, the sun is directly above the Equator, meaning night and day are of equal length. In solstice, the sun's path is at its furthest point from the Equator. Winter solstice is the shortest day of the year, while summer solstice is the longest. Witches, who live by the cycle of the sun and moon, celebrate Equinox and Solstice with spiritual rituals, such as creating trays or offerings, reading poems and meditating.

Casting spells

Casting a spell can help you to set your intentions and work towards your goals. You can source spells online or from books, or you can make your own basic ones. If you've ever made a wish over a birthday cake, you've cast a spell before. Think about your goal – for example, you may want to achieve greater self-acceptance. Summarise your desire in a few words – such as, 'I will learn to love and accept myself – then repeat your sentence in a way that feels meaningful to you. This might be writing it down, speaking to yourself in the mirror or rehearsing over candlelight.

Tarot reading

Tarot cards are a deck of seventy-eight cards that are used as a tool for divination. Each card has a meaning that can be applied

as a framework for understanding your intuition. Though there
is a complex structure to tarot readings, the basic format is as
follows: you ask an open-ended question to the deck of cards and
use the reading to guide you forward. For example, you may ask,
'What should I look for in a relationship?' or 'How can I move
away from feeling stressed?' You will then shuffle the deck and
pull one or multiple cards. Let the cards speak to your intuition
and guide you through your question. Tarot readings are a
useful tool for reflection and interpreting possibilities.

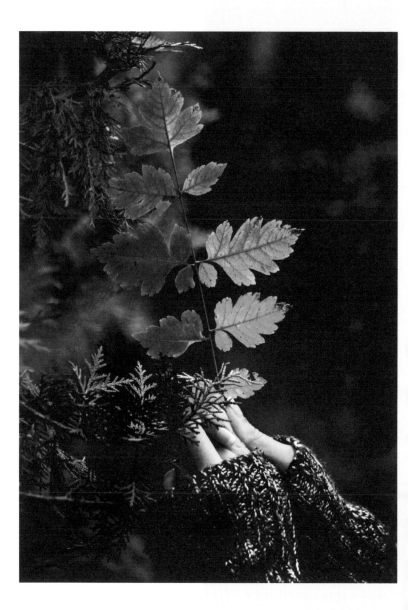

Enchantment

Cottagecore imagery often evokes a sense of enchantment and fairy tales. It is a form of escapism, but it also seeks to bring fantasy into the everyday and provide a real sense of wonder. There are plenty of ways to let a little bit of enchantment into your life; here are just a few.

Escape into fairytale locations

This might be a woodland walk, or a visit to an unspoiled historic village, a castle or even your local pumpkin patch. Any of these places can evoke a fairytale image. It might sound a little cheesy, but these locations can really get your imagination running wild, providing an alternative fantasy through which to escape from modern stress.

Nourish your inner child

As we grow older, we are increasingly laden with demands, chores and responsibilities. Under the weight of it all, it's easy to lose sight of your inner child. Think of the things that used to bring you joy – they are still pathways to happiness today. Try to let go of the idea that you're too old for something. If you want to jump in puddles on a rainy day, you go and enjoy it! Sing and dance to your favourite songs like nobody is watching, go on fairground rides and look forward to that packet of sweets.

'The world is full
of magic things
patiently waiting
for our senses
to grow sharper.'

– W. B. Yeats –

Cherish your hobbies

There is so much pressure to excel at a hobby that we can be put off trying it in the first place. There is also an expectation to monetise our hobbies, so that we can be the textbook definition of 'successful'. If you can defy these demands, and practise something simply for the love of doing it, it will bring you an uplifting sense of purpose and wonderment. If you are lucky enough to have a hobby already, cherish it and protect it from outside influences. If you haven't found one yet, allow yourself the space to try a new craft or experience without judgement or expectations. Crafts such as knitting, which involve repeating and rhythmic movements, can be incredibly calming.

Everyone is different, and there is no right or wrong way to let a bit of magick or enchantment into your life. Practising magick can help to provide the sense of escapism that is central to Cottagecore, while writing and casting spells can help you to focus on your goals and self-development. Experiment with the possibilities until you find a structure that works for you.

CULTURE

CULTURE

The desire to return to a simple way of living is everywhere. Where popular culture might have previously focused on hustle and the American dream, in places the emphasis is now on becoming more gentle and pastoral. Forget wealth and conventional success – our new aspirations are freedom, self-expression and a love of the natural world.

So those with a bookish streak might want to have a cozy evening curled up with a Jane Austen novel. If film is more your cup of tea, many classic tales have been bought to life on screen, and the elaborate artistry, set and costume design create a totally immersive and enchanting world that's sure to satisfy your penchant for Cottagecore. If you find yourself wanting some culture on the go, why not add a little magic to your journey with a Cottagecore playlist?

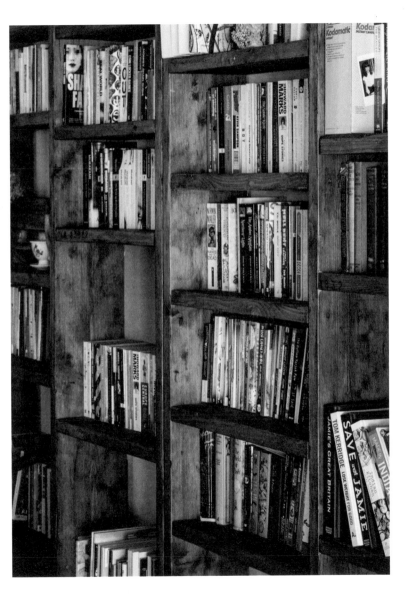

Music

Cottagecore playlists often appreciate indie folk artists, and songs that comment on the wilderness, fairy tales and emotional experiences. If you're in search of some new Cottagecore music, here are some artists to listen to:

Taylor Swift

American singer-songwriter Taylor Swift channelled Cottagecore's magic into her 2020 album, *Folklore*. Unlike her usual pop style, *Folklore* is a mellow album structured on gentle piano and guitar. Through her lyrics, she tells a collection of imagined stories, with recurring character arcs and themes of love, whimsy and escapism woven throughout the album. In true Cottagecore spirit, Swift described the writing process of *Folklore* as 'escaping into fantasy'.

Sufjan Stevens

Sufjan Stevens is an American singer, songwriter and multi-instrumentalist living in New York City. Stevens has a remarkable ability to move between instruments and themes, so his music is hard to tie down in one category, although it is often linked to indie folk or alternative rock. Songs such as 'Mystery of Love' and 'Should Have Known Better' are favourites among Cottagecore playlists, as they guide us gently through themes of love, grief and spirituality, providing a space to confront raw emotion.

Joanna Wang

A Taiwanese–American singer–songwriter, Joanna Wang is inspired by a mix of pop, video games and fairy tales. Covers like 'Alice in Wonderland', 'Moon River' and 'Pure Imagination' are sure to make you feel some Cottagecore magic.

Lord Huron

Lord Huron is an indie folk band based in Los Angeles. Lead artist, Ben Schneider, named the band after his childhood memories of visiting Lake Huron. The band is a tribute to escaping into the wilderness, finding freedom in nature and playing music around a campfire. Their first full-length album, *Lonesome Dreams*, is a collection of nostalgic adventure tales told through music. If you're looking for a Cottagecore road-trip playlist, start with Lord Huron.

Cottagecore playlist

* 'Cardigan' – Taylor Swift
* 'Meet Me In The Woods' – Lord Huron
* 'Alice in Wonderland' – Joanna Wang
* 'Mystery of Love' – Sufjan Stevens
* 'Fast Car' – Tracy Chapman
* 'The Secret Garden' – AURORA
* 'Youth' – Daughter
* 'Little Talks' – Of Monsters and Men
* 'Dog Days Are Over' – Florence + The Machine
* 'I Follow Rivers' – Lykke Li
* 'Sunlight' – Hozier
* 'Bloom' – The Paper Kites

Film

Cottagecore film lovers will most likely be drawn to modern
re-imaginings of classic literature – from their elaborate historic
costumes and styling to the picture-perfect locations, stripped of
all hints of modernity. Here are some recommendations for your
next movie night.

Little Women

The classic novel *Little Women* by Louisa May Alcott has been
retold through film in 1949, 1994 and 2019. All versions are
beautiful in their own right and deserve to be recommended.
The 2019 version has some especially breathtaking scenery,
effects and costume design. We follow the four March sisters as
they chase their dreams, in spite of life's hardships. Within no
time, you feel like you are part of their family, sharing every step
of their emotional journey.

Moonrise Kingdom

A Cottagecore film guide would not be complete without a little
Wes Anderson. *Moonrise Kingdom* tells the story of adolescent love,
and the desire to escape the stresses of modern life by running
away into the wilderness. With classic Wes Anderson artistry,
dreamy pastel hues and perfectly styled Sixties' outfits and props,
this is a film that will inspire your creative side.

'I declare after all there is no enjoyment like reading! How much sooner one tires of any thing than of a book! – When I have a house of my own, I shall be miserable if I have not an excellent library.'

– Jane Austen –

Pride and Prejudice

There have been a number of adaptations of Jane Austen's
Pride and Prejudice, including a 1995 TV series and a 2005 film.
There has been ongoing debate among fans as to which of
these two versions most does the novel justice, though they
are both wonderful in different ways. The 2005 version
features Keira Knightley as Elizabeth Bennet, and includes
fabulous Cottagecore-esque locations, including Groombridge
Place, Chatsworth House and Stourhead, brought to life with
breathtaking cinematography. Those with an eye for historic
fashion will also enjoy the Regency costumes. There is a lot to
be inspired by.

Other Cottagecore film recommendations

* *Fairytale: A True Story* (1997)

* *Picnic at Hanging Rock* (1975)

* *A Room With a View* (1985)

* *My Neighbor Totoro* (1988)

* *The Secret Garden* (1993 & 2020)

* *Mary and the Witch's Flower* (2017)

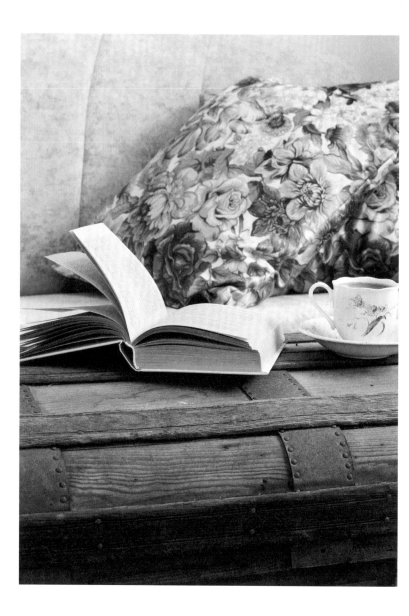

Reading

You can always count on a classic if you want to cosy up under a duvet with a book. Here are a few you can try if you want to escape into a fantasyland of nature and whimsy.

The Secret Garden

This novel by Frances Hodgson Burnett has remained a favourite among children since it was published in 1911. Set in England, the novel's overarching theme is the rejuvenating power of nature. As the characters spend more time in the natural landscape, their health and imaginations flourish, and as nature cares for them, they, in turn, care for the secret garden. It is a whimsical tale of friendship and magic – a classic not to miss.

Alice's Adventures in Wonderland

Chances are you are already familiar with the modern adaptations of *Alice in Wonderland*. The original work, *Alice's Adventures in Wonderland*, is a novel by Lewis Carroll, published in 1865. We follow Alice on a journey into a fantasy land, where she meets an assortment of interesting creatures. The novel brings a deeper experience of childhood innocence, and pokes fun at the arbitrary and sometimes unnecessary complexities of adult life. It is a reminder to listen to our inner child.

Wuthering Heights

Written by Emily Brontë and published in 1847, *Wuthering Heights* is often cited as the greatest love story, although it doesn't portray love in the way you might expect. Love in *Wuthering Heights* is wild, psychotic and haunting. This book is raw and eerie, inspired by the landscape of the Yorkshire moors.

Five more books to add to your Cottagecore reading list

1. *Anne of Green Gables* by L. M. Montgomery
2. *The Wind in the Willows* by Kenneth Grahame
3. *World of Wonders: In Praise of Fireflies, Whale Sharks, and Other Astonishments* by Aimee Nezhukumatathil
4. *The Secret Life of Bees* by Sue Monk Kidd
5. *Little House in the Big Woods* by Laura Ingalls Wilder

There are plenty of vintage works to provide the backbone to Cottagecore culture. Now, as we reinvent what it means to embrace pastoral aspects of life, there are lots of modern interpretations of Cottagecore too.

ENTERTAINING

ENTERTAINING

Once you've welcomed Cottagecore into your own experience, why not share the joy with your loved ones, too? Cottagecore is about connection, be it with nature, with yourself or with your loved ones. To host the perfect Cottagecore get-together, think all things whimsy and pastoral. A picnic nestled amongst the trees, an assortment of eclectic vintage props, a centrepiece of homemade baked goods and, most importantly, the company of treasured friends. With a bit of preparation, you can create a tea party fit for a fairy tale.

So from a quiet cup of herbal tea with a friend to an elaborate garden party with a welcome crowd, here are some ways to come together in true Cottagecore spirit.

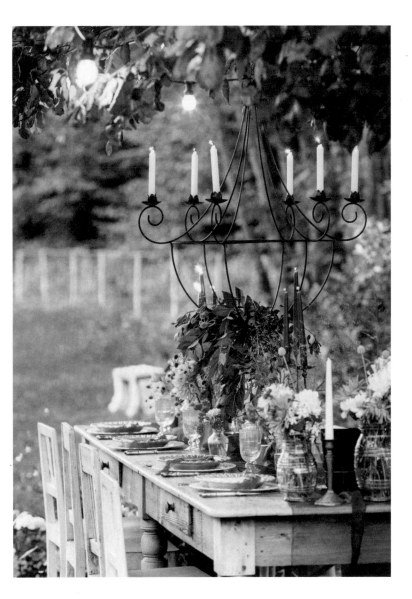

Baking

Sharing homemade cake is a win-win. Not only do you get to enjoy the comfort and nostalgia of baking, you also get to show your loved ones you care.

Honey And Almond Cake

This honey and almond cake is delicious with a cup of tea, or makes a fabulous centrepiece for a grander occasion.

Serves 8 · Prep 15 minutes · Cooking time 35–40 minutes

185g (6½oz/¾ cups) almond butter

125g (4oz/generous ½ cup) butter, at room temperature

180ml (6½fl oz/¾ cup) clear honey, plus extra for drizzling

2 medium free-range eggs, beaten

125g (4½oz/1¼ cups) plain (all-purpose) flour

1 tsp baking powder

½ tsp bicarbonate of soda (baking soda)

½ tsp salt

75g (3oz/½ cup) ground almonds (almond meal)

3–4 tbsp flaked (slivered) almonds

1. Preheat the oven to 180°C (160°C fan)/350°F/gas 4. Line a 20cm (8in) loose-bottomed tin (springform pan) with baking parchment.

2. Using a food mixer or hand-held electric whisk, beat the almond butter, butter and honey until smooth and well combined. Whisk in the beaten eggs.

3. Sift the flour, baking powder and bicarbonate of soda into the mixture. Add the salt and ground almonds and fold in gently with a metal spoon in a figure-of-eight motion, until everything is incorporated evenly.

4. Spoon the mixture into the lined baking tin and sprinkle the flaked almonds over the top. Bake in the preheated oven for 35–40 minutes, until the cake is risen and golden brown and springs back when you press it gently. To test whether it's cooked, insert a metal skewer into the centre – if it comes out clean, it's ready.

5. Leave to cool in the tin for 10 minutes before turning out on to a wire rack. Drizzle some honey over the warm cake and leave until it's completely cold and has absorbed the honey. Cut into slices to serve. Store in a tin or airtight container for up to 5 days.

How to throw
a tea party

A tea party is a wonderful way to celebrate a birthday or special occasion. You may wish for a simple tea-and-scones affair, or perhaps you want to go full blown into Alice-in-Wonderland territory.

First, assess the basic structure. If you are blessed with good weather, make sure you have picnic rugs and a hamper to stage your tea party. An outdoor table and chairs also make for an enchanting outdoor setting, particularly if you have a vintage metal or wooden set. Consider covering your table with a crisp white tablecloth if you are hosting a formal event, or a chintzy floral fabric for a more relaxed vibe.

Next up is crockery. The quintessential set-up here is the three-tier plate stand, a large teapot, accompanied by individual teacups and saucers and finally, a set of vintage cutlery. If you don't have a plate stand, a selection of mismatched vintage plates can be just as charming. Chances are, you'll be able to find a good selection in a second-hand store.

You will probably find that a lot of your table or picnic-rug space is occupied with food and drink, so decorations can be kept simple – a jug of fresh or dried flowers is perfect.

When it comes to the food, the menu for a full afternoon tea usually consists of savoury finger sandwiches (no crusts!), scones with cream and jam and a platter of sweets including jellies, fruits and miniature cakes. For a lighter or more informal setting, stick with scones, cream and jam.

Food should be accompanied by tea. You can get creative here. There are plenty of gorgeously fragranced loose-leaf teas to choose from. Classic teas for the occasion include Earl Grey, Assam and chamomile, but why not also try some floral ones, such as lavender, rose or elderflower?

If you are celebrating a special occasion, accompany your afternoon tea with a garden punch or rosé cocktail. The following recipes may give you some inspiration:

Gardener's Punch

Serves 7

125g (4oz/½ cup) caster sugar

120ml (4fl oz/½ cup) water

10g (¼oz/½ cup) fresh basil

750ml (26fl oz/3 cups) chilled London dry gin

250ml (8½fl oz/1 cup) chilled peach schnapps

750ml (26fl oz/3 cups) chilled peach nectar

250ml (8½fl oz/1 cup) freshly squeezed lime juice

1 litre (34fl oz/4¼ cups) chilled soda water

Lime slices, peach slices, raspberries, basil and mint leaves, to garnish

1. Start by making a basil syrup: combine the sugar and water in a small saucepan. Gently heat, stirring until the sugar dissolves. Bring to the boil, then turn down the heat and simmer for 2 minutes. Take off the heat, drop in the basil and leave to cool and infuse. When the syrup is cold, strain it into a sterilised jar, discarding the basil, then seal and store in the fridge for up to 2 weeks.

2. Pour all the basil syrup into a large jug or punch bowl. Add the gin, peach schnapps, peach nectar and lime juice and stir to mix well. Top up with soda water. Add slices of lime and peach, a few handfuls of raspberries and a couple of handfuls of basil and mint leaves.

3. Give it a gentle stir, then pour or ladle into punch glasses, with ice on hand for people who want their punch a little chilled.

Sloe Gin Fizz

Serves 1

50g (2oz) caster sugar

50ml (2fl oz) water

60ml (2fl oz) sloe gin

30ml (1fl oz) freshly squeezed
lemon juice

Soda water, to top up

A lemon wedge and mint sprig,
to garnish

1. Start by making the sugar syrup: combine the sugar and water
in a small saucepan. Gently heat, stirring until the sugar dissolves.
Bring to the boil, then turn down the heat and simmer for
2 minutes. When the syrup is cold, pour it into a sterilised
jar, seal and store in the fridge for up to 2 weeks.

2. Pour the sloe gin, lemon juice and 8ml (¼fl oz) of the simple syrup
into an ice-filled cocktail shaker. Shake together well.

3. Fill a tall glass with ice, strain in the gin mix, then top up with
soda water for the fizz. Garnish with the wedge of lemon and sprig
of fresh mint.

English 75

Serves 1

45ml (1½fl oz) Earl Grey gin
½ tbsp elderflower cordial
1 tbsp freshly squeezed
lemon juice

75ml (2½fl oz/⅓ cup) English
sparkling wine, chilled

1. Fill a shaker with ice and pour in the gin, elderflower cordial and lemon juice. Shake together vigorously, then strain into a flute.

2. Carefully pour in half the sparkling wine and give it a little stir, then top up with the rest of the sparkling wine and serve.

Sweet Honey Rosé

Serves 1

1 tbsp honey
1 tbsp water
45ml (1½fl oz) whisky

Splash of lemon juice
45ml (1½fl oz) rosé

1. There are no secrets to making honey syrup: combine the honey and water and stir until you get a uniform consistency. It's a simple trick that thins out the honey, just enough to make it easier to mix in cold drinks.

2. Combine all the ingredients in a cocktail shaker filled with ice. Shake well and strain into a chilled cocktail glass.

Decorating ideas

Once you've got your menu planned, it's time to start setting the scene. Try some of the following decoration ideas to set a perfect Cottagecore mood for entertaining your loved ones.

Bunting

You can decorate the edge of your table or the surrounding area with a row of bunting, which often comes in floral or chintz patterns, making it perfect for a cottage-inspired party.

Centrepieces

A centrepiece brings your tablescape together by providing a focal point. If you are serving cake or dessert, you could use this, until it's time to eat it. A tall cake standing on a rustic log or wooden crate is a classic example. Alternatively, you could try a floral arrangement, or a three-tier cake stand decorated with pine cones and foliage.

Lighting

If your event is taking place in the evening, you'll want to think about lighting. Thankfully there are many gorgeous ways to light your scene. Well-designed lighting can have a magical effect on the mood. Why not try some of the following?

If your table is positioned under a tree, you could suspend a hanging candle chandelier from a branch above.

Get creative with outdoor fairy lights. Hang them so that they flow between trees, along a balcony or even suspend them from a washing line or fence post.

Adorn the table with lanterns, candelabra or jam jars filled with tea lights.

Placeholders

If you are hosting more than a couple of guests, it helps to mark people's spaces at the table with placeholders. These can be super simple. Take a small piece of card and write your guest's name in calligraphy (if you struggle with this, you can print the names with a pretty font instead). Punch a hole through the top of the card, thread some twine through the hole and finish with a little bow. You could also thread a small piece of foliage through the bow for a rustic finish.

Place mats

If you are going for a stripped-back, rustic mood, you can use neutral linen place mats, or another natural material, such as cork or wool. If you are going for more of a happily cluttered look, use floral chintz fabric for a bit of cottage charm. The same rules apply if you are using a table runner.

Napkin holders

You may be able to pick up some vintage brass-style napkin holders if you're lucky in the second-hand store. Otherwise, vintage replicas should be available in homeware stores and online. You can create a simple napkin holder by tying a piece of twine around a rolled napkin, finishing it with a bow, and then threading a small piece of foliage through the bow.

Table decorations

Thankfully, vintage table decorations are easy to come by when either shopping second hand or going on a woodland walk. Look for the following items, and don't worry if they are mismatched – that only adds to the charm:

* Moss
* Pine cones
* Foliage – pine branches are good for this
* Leaves
* Flowers, either loose or in small glass jars to hold upright
* Vintage books
* Assorted vintage drinks glasses

There are plenty of ways to throw a Cottagecore gathering. Next time you are due to celebrate a friend's birthday, why not host a garden party instead of going out for drinks?

FINAL THOUGHTS

Cottagecore is a place where we can escape the chaos of modern life. Sure, it's a bit of a fantasy for most of us. But that isn't a reason not to indulge in it. In fact, all the more reason for it! When we get wrapped up in the dull monotony of working all week, the best thing we can do to lift our spirits is to indulge in a playful, imaginative state and nourish our inner child.

As much as Cottagecore is booming online, it's important to take a few steps away and disconnect from social media. Spend some time in a green space, feel the earth beneath your feet as you walk through the grass, pay attention to what you can see and hear around you, and form a strong memory that you can revisit when you need to. Breathe. Take a moment to re-engage your connection with nature, and to disengage from your online connections.

When we do share our Cottagecore moments online, that is still valid escapism. If you are proud of a pie you baked or you saw a beautiful view on a hike and want to share it with your followers, go ahead and celebrate it, making space for joy. Cottagecore isn't about returning to a technology-free era and living off the land. It's a modern balance. In an ideal world, you can enjoy social media and sharing the positive or real moments, yet notice when your phone isn't serving you; then it's time to unplug and engage in something cathartic – whether that's enjoying a craft like knitting or taking a break outside.

Getting in touch with the simple pleasures doesn't have to be covered in frills. It can be straightforward. Yet it can also be radical. You can step away from commercialism in different areas of your life. You might choose to upcycle some planters instead of going to the garden centre for new ones. Perhaps you'll start buying your produce from the farmers' market instead of the supermarket. Maybe you'll add a patch of vintage fabric to your ripped jeans to keep them going for another year. These simple acts are freeing in so many ways. We can take pleasure in the literal act of making something. But we can go one step further, and appreciate the money saved or diverted away from big businesses by repurposing what would otherwise go to waste, and the resources we avoided exploiting by not buying something new.

By taking these small steps, we are saying no to consumerism and mass production where we can. We are celebrating the alternatives of handmade crafts, makers and artisans, upcycling, second-hand shopping and building things to last. There is a place in between minimalism and consumerism where we may buy just enough (from small businesses or ethical brands), cherish our belongings, repair our damaged goods, pot up plants for pollinators, follow more plant-based and seasonal diets and share things when we no longer have a use for them. In fact, we were already doing a lot of these things before the Industrial Revolution. There's no reason why we can't learn to value them again. You don't have to do it all, nor do you need to do things perfectly. Cottagecore is about living a little slower and with greater intention.

The bigger picture is that we reduce our burden on the world's resources. We look out for the environment and we recognise that as we look out for nature, it looks out for us too. It is a two-way relationship, and the key is in the balance of both give and take.

Importantly, Cottagecore holds space for everybody. As a movement that was started by the LGBTQIA+ community, it's vital not to lose sight of the original vision. Cottagecore is a safe space from a world that thinks in oppressive categories and binaries. It's a place where experiences are heard and honoured, and mistreatment is not welcome. It is a retreat, where you can escape from hardship and nourish yourself, while the rest of the world catches up. If you find the space to heal, you will be stronger when you return.

There is no checklist to prove your worthiness here. At its most straightforward level, Cottagecore is enjoying your commute outside, or getting excited over your new houseplant. You might be dreaming about moving to a historic home in the countryside one day, but you might also not! You are allowed to appreciate the city and the countryside, or one and not the other. It's your vision, and you can shape it in a way that best meets your needs.

Have fun experimenting with something new or returning to a lost family tradition. Savour the experience and learn to see meaning outside of conventional wealth and productivity. There is value in existing, observing and feeling. Get carried away with the fantasy and enjoy your escape into Cottagecore.

Acknowledgements

Thank you to the team at HarperCollins for your help in putting this book together, particularly Omara for your in-depth guidance and encouragement along the way.

I am forever grateful to my grandad, who showed me the escapism within nature and gardening from an early age.

Thank you to my wonderful partner Aaron and my friends Kym, Tor, Rach, Amy, K and Andy. Last but not least, thank you to my family – Dad, Kiara, Sue, Shane and the Wilsons.

About the Author

Ramona is an influencer and photographer from Somerset, England. She documents cottage life and the English countryside on her Instagram account, @monalogue. In her spare time you'll find her in the garden, where she grows a variety of vegetables and cut flowers. Ramona graduated from the University of Bristol with a degree in Experimental Psychology.